THE NIGHTMARE
WAS JUST BEGINNING...

In the dim yellow light of the van, Denise saw the man go back to his shelves. Things were getting hazy now. She couldn't think straight. He came back with something in his hands. It was long. Yellow and white. A cord. What, she thought, what is this? She was fading away, a loud rushing noise in her ears, her eyes slipping out of focus.

She was still half-conscious when he pushed her down on the floor and climbed on top of her. I'm dying, she thought vaguely. I will never wake up from this night.

Before she passed out, her last thought was that something even more terrible was about to happen to her.

SIGNET ONYX

INCREDIBLE—BUT TRUE CRIME

☐ **SLEEP MY CHILD, FOREVER The Riveting True Story of a Mother Who Murdered Her Own Children by John Coston.** Without evidence of any kind, physical or medical, Detective Sergeant Joseph Burgoon of the St. Louis homicide division, slowly unraveled a labyrinth of deceptions and lies to reveal Ellen Boehm as a cold-blooded killer who couldn't wait to collect on the large insurance policies she had secretly taken out on her children. (403355—$5.99)

☐ **MOMMIE'S LITTLE ANGELS The True Story of a Mother Who Murdered Seven Children by Mary Lou Cavenaugh.** Here is the riveting story of Diana Lumbrera, the most monstrous mom since Diane Downs, who left a trail of tiny corpses from Texas to Kansas. (404939—$5.99)

☐ **PRECIOUS VICTIMS:** *A True Story of Motherly Love and Murder* **by Don W. Weber and Charles Bosworth, Jr.** Who would believe a mother would kill her two-week-old baby? Here is the terrifying story of the twisted hate that seethed below the surface of a seemingly normal family. (171845—$5.99)

*Prices slightly higher in Canada

Buy them at your local bookstore or use this convenient coupon for ordering.

PENGUIN USA
P.O. Box 999 — Dept. #17109
Bergenfield, New Jersey 07621

Please send me the books I have checked above.
I am enclosing $_____ (please add $2.00 to cover postage and handling). Send check or money order (no cash or C.O.D.'s) or charge by Mastercard or VISA (with a $15.00 minimum). Prices and numbers are subject to change without notice.

Card #_____ Exp. Date _____
Signature_____
Name_____
Address_____
City _____ State _____ Zip Code _____

For faster service when ordering by credit card call **1-800-253-6476**

Allow a minimum of 4-6 weeks for delivery. This offer is subject to change without notice.

DEADLY THRILLS

Jaye Slade Fletcher

AN ONYX BOOK

ONYX
Published by the Penguin Group
Penguin Books USA Inc., 375 Hudson Street,
New York, New York 10014, U.S.A.
Penguin Books Ltd, 27 Wrights Lane,
London W8 5TZ, England
Penguin Books Australia Ltd, Ringwood,
Victoria, Australia
Penguin Books Canada Ltd, 10 Alcorn Avenue,
Toronto, Ontario, Canada M4V 3B2
Penguin Books (N.Z.) Ltd, 182–190 Wairau Road,
Auckland 10, New Zealand

Penguin Books Ltd, Registered Offices:
Harmondsworth, Middlesex, England

First published by Onyx, an imprint of Dutton Signet,
a division of Penguin Books USA Inc.

First Printing, September, 1995
10 9 8 7 6 5 4 3 2 1

Copyright © Jaye Slade Fletcher, 1995
All rights reserved

Printed in the United States of America

To Eric,
my very special son

ACKNOWLEDGMENTS

To all of the police personnel, prosecutors, and judges named in the book, I salute you for removing these truly evil men from our society, and I thank you for all your time and courtesy to me. We have spent many hundreds of hours together, poring over details.

Others who are not named in the book gave freely of their time and expertise to help me with this four-year project. Many Chicago suburban chiefs of police, sergeants, detectives and police officers spent time with me and were generous with their information and advice. Specifically, I thank Lisa Howard, Renee Goldfarb of the Cook County State's Attorney's Office, Nic Howell of the Illinois Department of Corrections, veteran *Sun-Times* police reporters Jim Casey and Tom Frisbee, the friends of Bill W., and Ms. Sarah McDermott, who was there for me during the last days of panic.

Thanks to Wayne Klatt and Gary Provost

for all the editorial assistance, and to my lovely agent, Susan Crawford, who stayed by me when things were at their darkest and who was still there when the lights went back on.

My special gratitude is reserved for Elmhurst Chief of Police John Millner. I am a Chicago girl, and when I began to research The Ripper Crew's crimes in the Western suburbs I was lost. Chief Millner made phone calls for me and provided introductions to sources I could not otherwise have reached.

The parents, families, and friends of the victims opened their hearts and homes to me, sharing memories of their now-lost young ladies. For them the years have passed but the pain has not.

Finally, my thanks to my sisters and my friends, who've heard more about serial killers in these past years than they ever wanted to know.

Prologue

Tina hung up the phone. She closed her eyes and took a deep breath. A familiar rush of excitement washed over her. He was on his way over.

She waddled into the bathroom, her pregnant belly huge and drooping. She fixed her face and brushed her hair, and then stood back to study the effect. I look like a cow, she thought. She prodded the puffiness around her cheeks and chin. But then she smiled. He wouldn't care, wouldn't even notice. He liked her like this, her breasts heavy and full, her face and thighs padded. "A real woman," he called her.

Please, Lord, she thought, don't let him be in one of his mean moods. Let him be nice again, like he used to be.

When the red van pulled up a few minutes later, Tina rushed to the door to meet him. She smiled and held out her arms, but he had what she thought of as "that look" on his face, that staring, wide-blue, glazed look, and her heart started pounding. Oh, no, not again, please.

She started to say, "Hi, honey," but before the words were even out of her mouth he rushed at her. Grabbing her breasts in both hands, he slammed her back against the wall. Then he squeezed. And twisted. Hard. Tina gasped, closing her eyes against the pain and going limp, the way he liked her.

"Are you going to do it for me?" he asked.

"No, I can't!" she cried. "Please don't ask me anymore!"

"Just one nipple, that's all I'm asking," he said soothingly. "I just want to see inside, see how they work."

He gave a vicious pinch, and Tina felt hot tears flow from her eyes. She shook her head back and forth. This same conversation, this same craziness, all these months. And it was getting worse.

Finally, he pushed her away and walked past her into the kitchen. Tina brushed at her eyes. She took deep breaths, trying to get her heart to quiet down. Maybe his wife is right, she thought. Maybe he really is going crazy.

She had confronted his wife months earlier, and the two women, both so much in love with the same man, had established an uneasy friendship.

His wife, pale and sweating and obviously ill, had shown Tina the long straight pins in her breasts that he had forced her to endure, confessing that he had injected her with drugs to stave off the pain and infection. She had told Tina about his having sex with her parents' big white dog. "Right in their living room," she had said. She had shown Tina his underwear, all the coarse white hairs. The two women had been joined by their fear.

Now Tina went into the kitchen. He was sitting at the table, a beer in hand. He stared at her, his eyes like blue marbles.

"If you really love me," he said flatly, "you'll cut off one of your nipples and let me see inside. It's no big deal, really. Black hookers do it all the time."

"No," she whispered, weary now, and so afraid. It had been their only conversation for many months.

Suddenly he stood up, knocking his beer to the floor. Tina shrank back against the wall. "All right!" he shouted. "If you won't do it for me, I'll find someone who will!" He rushed past her and out the door.

It was April 1981.

Chapter One

At 11:15 on the warm, drizzly morning of June 1, 1981, detectives Warren Wilkosz and John Sam of the DuPage County Sheriff's Department drove to the Moonlit Motel in the unincorporated area of Villa Park. They had gotten a call. A woman's body had been found.

When they got to the motel, Wilkosz pulled into the parking lot and stared out at the dismal, rain-smeared building. White paint was peeling from the clapboard walls of the dingy L-shaped structure. Behind the dirty windowpanes cheap curtains hung closed, as if to hide lurid secrets.

"Ah, yes, folks," Detective Sam muttered, "the Bates Motel."

Every cop in DuPage County was familiar with the Moonlit. It had been known for many years as the local "hot-pillow joint," a place where rooms were rented for a few hours of illicit sex. There had been rumors about the Moonlit Motel since long before Wilkosz came on the scene. People said that back in 1962 a murdered baby was found in one of the rooms. Wild parties seemed to go on in there around the clock. Beer bashes tended to get out of hand, bottles being tossed and knives pulled. And every once in a while an adulterer would get caught at the motel, sparking a three-way fight that frequently turned physical and spilled out into the street. The police were called to come out to the motel nearly every week for one sort of disturbance or another.

"It was a joke around the department that the sheriff should open a branch office at the Moonlit," Wilkosz says.

The motel is situated on the North Avenue strip, a bleak mile-long stretch of struggling auto-repair places, donut shops, and fast-food outlets, where the air carries an uneasy blend of damp rust, exhaust fumes, and hamburger grease. Used-car lots dot the strip with their garish, blinking signs that advertise: NO CREDIT NEEDED, and gluey blots of dusted-over oil stain the driveways. The locals call it the Gaza Strip.

Waiting for Wilkosz and Sam on this rainy morning was Hank McGinnis, manager of the motel. He was a lanky, stoop-shouldered, gloomy man, right out of central casting.

"The maid complained of a bad smell coming from somewhere 'round back," McGinnis told the detectives. "I didn't know what to make of it at first. People *will* get up to all sorts of stuff in them rooms. I can never tell from one day to the next what'all I'm gonna find, you know?"

McGinnis looked expectantly from one detective to the other, his dour face brightening a bit at the hope the detectives were going to show some interest in his motel room gossip. Wilkosz and Sam stood in the drizzling rain, looking at McGinnis, saying nothing.

The motel manager cleared his throat. "Yeah, well, anyway, as I was saying, yesterday the maid says that smell's getting worse, so I come out here and took me a look around, you know?"

Warren Wilkosz took out his notebook and a gold Cross pen. "And?"

McGinnis said he had gone out into the weedy field behind the motel. There he had smelled the stench, thick and rotten and oddly sweet. He had moved quickly, holding his hand to his nose between gulps of air, kicking aside crushed beer cans and broken bottles, all the time thinking he would come upon a dead cat or raccoon, or perhaps a deer that had wandered into the path of a westbound truck.

What he found instead was the body of a young woman.

"That's when I called you guys," he told the detectives.

They headed around to the rear of the building. "Did you touch the body?" Sam asked.

McGinnis gaped, clearly insulted. "Well, hell, 'course I didn't touch the body! Don't I watch all them cop shows just like everybody else? Besides," he smirked, "wait'll you get a look at this. Ain't nobody this side of a loony bin going to be touching what's out in that field unless they absolutely got no choice about it."

Wilkosz and Sam, like most detectives, had seen more than their share of human damage in all its forms. Sometimes people managed to slip away into death still cloaked in a bit of dignity. But mostly, like this one, they did not.

The girl's body was nearly a skeleton. Infested with maggots, she lay facedown in the field, her arms bound behind her with cheap nickel-plated handcuffs. Wilkosz noticed that a broken fragment of the cuff key was still imbedded in the lock.

The two men made their preliminary "eyeball investigation," as it's called, then stood up and stepped back a few paces, taking in the death scene as a whole. Hank McGinnis, behind them, peered around for a last look and then, shaking his head and holding his nose, he headed back inside the motel.

"So, what do you make of it?" Wilkosz said. In the way of most longtime police partners, they would each toss out first impressions, initial "maybes" and "what ifs" so that their individual perspectives could blend together, forming a more complete picture than either man could have come up with alone.

"Well," John Sam mused, "she's been dead awhile."

"Spoken like a rookie," Wilkosz teased, and both men smiled at the remark as they continued to study the scene. Animal flesh, whether human or otherwise, takes time to degenerate. And carnivorous insects, Mother Nature's cleaning crew, take time to get down to business. This body had been nearly skeletonized by a host invasion of parasites, and what was left of the flesh was badly broken down, on its way toward falling off the bones.

Warren Wilkosz was the department's senior detective. John Sam, coming from the patrol division, had made detective the year before, and the two men had worked together since. They had formed a comfortable working relationship. Wilkosz, a tall, intense look-alike for actor William Hurt, was perfectly suited for the profession of homicide detective because of his inherently suspicious nature. He believed a thing only when he could prove it, and the questions were always in his eyes, "Is that true?" and "What's the real story behind this?" A newspaper columnist once observed that police officers seem to have two sets of eyes, one behind the other, so that on the surface they are looking at you and listening to you, while behind that they are internally scanning through their own vast knowledge of humanity's baser instincts, and working out just where in that catalogue you fit.

Wilkosz gave great attention to his working appearance, favoring muted-toned cashmere sportcoats with leather patches at the elbows, knife-creased trousers, and soft, hand-stitched loafers of Italian or Spanish leather. He wore gold-rimmed glasses, a gold wedding ring, and a gold watch, but the intensity of his nature showed through when he took out his gold pen to write, for he pressed so hard that the point nearly bore through the paper, leaving a clear, raised impression on the reverse side. His colleagues described Wilkosz in one word—relentless. "If I was one of the bad guys," a fellow detective said, "I wouldn't want Warren on my trail. The man is utterly relentless, as though an unsolved crime is a personal affront to him. Catching killers for a living is a mean, ugly game of wits and stealth, and it's a game Warren means to win every single time."

John Sam was a slim, slight-statured man. Trim and prematurely silver-haired, he was a good detective, but he was having difficulty adjusting to what he viewed as unwarranted political intrusion into police matters in upscale, politically powerful DuPage County. His unhappiness over this issue was certainly not unique; it has always been a cause of distress to career police officers. Just as Julius Caesar used his popularity with his armed troops to catapult himself to world domination, politicians since then have tried to use the police in one way or another, to propel themselves into the public forum and remain there.

The majority of decisions made by a career police officer involve the use of his own personal judgment. The police point of view is that such decisions should be made purely from a standpoint of justice and solid law enforcement standards, no matter the ramifications; the political point of view leans toward the importance of overall image, even if to the detriment of an individual case. The divergent views inevitably clash.

The two detectives paced around the body, studying the crime scene from different angles. The girl might once have been pretty, Wilkosz thought. She might have been someone's girlfriend, someone's mother. How old was she? he wondered. In death, it was hard to tell. Her black hair had fallen loose from her skull. He leaned down to touch it. It was a braided hairpiece, woven into her own short hair. Her left ear was double-pierced with two small yellow metal studs.

John Sam pulled on latex gloves and moved the corpse's head to one side. There wasn't much of a face left. She had a strip of unidentifiable cloth stuffed into her mouth.

"She was gagged," he said.

"Let the coroner remove it," Wilkosz said.

The woman was wearing a red, white, and blue-striped sweater, but no skirt or slacks. Her striped panties were pulled down over her thighs. She was wearing socks, but her shoes were missing. Although she was clothed, the upper portion of her torso was so decayed that it looked as if she had been dead for many weeks.

John Sam gingerly reached into a small bulge in the woman's sock. "Thirteen bucks," he said. "A ten and three singles." The detectives also noted that there were three pennies lying on the soggy ground next to the body, and that her cheap plastic-faced watch had stopped at 9:08. They didn't try to make sense of any of these things. At this point their job was simply to see everything, to make sure they didn't miss anything that might seem irrelevant now, but which might later prove to be vital evidence.

"What's your take on the time?" Sam asked.

"I don't know, what do you think? A month or so? Longer, maybe," Wilkosz answered. He leaned down and worked his gloved fingers into the ground beneath the body. It was muddy, damp. Before today's rain the last precipitation had been Friday night, when a summer storm deluged the western suburbs with nearly four inches of rain.

"Maybe she was killed somewhere else and dumped here later," Sam said now. "After the ground was already soaked from Friday's rain."

"Could be," Wilkosz answered, but then he shook his head. "But if we look at it that way, we have some problems with it. She wasn't dragged here, right? I mean, there's no trail of smashed-down weeds, so she must have been carried. And who in hell would carry a body in this condition?" They continued to puzzle over the probable circumstances of the woman's arrival in the field.

"Maybe," John Sam suggested, "she was killed in the motel a month ago, or whenever, and carried out here at night and dumped. And maybe"—he looked queasy at the thought—"the ground under her isn't wet from rain but from leaking body fluids." Both men looked down at their hands, grateful for the latex gloves.

Wilkosz told Sam to stay with the crime scene while he walked back to the motel to talk to the manager and phone the coroner's office. The coroner would notify one of the local funeral homes to send a hearse out to remove the body. Ordinarily, autopsies would be done at a local hospital, but in cases like this one, known in police circles as a "stinker," the odor and probable infectiousness of the body were simply too overwhelming. The body would be transported to the enormous county garage in Wheaton for autopsy.

Later that day at the garage, a stainless steel table and other equipment was placed over a large floor drain equipped with constantly running water. The massive overhead doors of the garage were opened, and gigantic floor fans, ordinarily used to clear away automobile exhaust fumes, were turned on full-blast. Only then could Deputy Coroner Pete Siekman perform the autopsy.

The next day, in his office at the county courthouse in Wheaton, Wilkosz sat at his desk, reviewing the case and thinking about how to find out more about the woman. The

violent-crimes office was small, no larger than a living room, and crammed with stark, functional gray metal desks, chairs, and file cabinets—used furniture that had been donated by Illinois Bell Telephone Company when they refurnished their own offices. The detectives described the office as "right out of *Barney Miller* and furnished with Ma Bell rejects."

Wilkosz pored through the DuPage County missing-persons' reports. He found nothing that fit a description of the woman. She could have come from another county, he thought. Or she might have been a runaway, or a prostitute with no family to report her missing. Wilkosz was frustrated. If that was so, there was little chance that he could wind up the case before his annual vacation, which was coming up soon. In fact, he thought, this might turn out to be one of those cases he most hated, the kind that never get solved. If she had been a hooker, she might have been killed for any number of reasons, and a hooker's acquaintances are usually not the type to step forward and volunteer information, or to leave a forwarding address. No, his best hope for a lead would be the autopsy results and dental comparison charts.

Meanwhile, on the off chance that she might be a hooker from Chicago, Wilkosz put a call in to Chicago's Area Five Detective Division, which covers that city's far west and northwest neighborhoods. He talked with Area Five Detective Mike Herigodt, and described the circumstances of the case: the body in the field behind the motel, the braided hairpiece, handcuffs, and money in the sock.

"Aha," said Herigodt, "money in her socks? You probably do have a Chicago hooker out there, my friend. The 'working girls,' as they call themselves, have been doing that lately—putting their money in their socks to keep from being ripped off by some john or street junkie. If you think about it, it makes sense, doesn't it? Where else are they going to put it? They don't carry purses, and everywhere else on their body is subject to inspection, if you know what I mean."

Herigodt explained that in Chicago, those hookers who worked for a pimp usually had their man standing by somewhere close while they made their deals. They would then turn the money over to their man before conducting their business. But girls working alone had no such backup protection. Herigodt told Wilkosz about one local Chicago legend, "Mailbox Marilyn," who carried a packet of self-addressed stamped envelopes around with her. When she got money from a trick, she would put it in an envelope and drop it into a mailbox, ensuring that even if the police did happen upon her in the middle of a "business session," she could not be charged with prostitution. The law defining prostitution contains two elements: one, a sex act; and two, exchange of money. Without the cash factor such goings-on merely constitute public indecency.

Detective Herigodt told Wilkosz that he didn't know of any similar Chicago cases, and certainly no outstanding crime patterns that fit the handcuffed DuPage victim, but he promised to get back to him if he ran across anything. The two men exchanged numbers and hung up, neither of them knowing at the time that this case was to be only the first in a pattern of grisly murders of Chicago-area women that would later be described as "the worst in the history of the Midwest."

Chapter Two

On June 12 Wilkosz and Sam climbed the shadowy stairway to a small apartment on West End Street in Chicago. They moved slowly. This was no emergency; today they were not the cavalry riding to the rescue. No, this was another part of the job, perhaps the hardest part. They were here to tell a mother that her child was dead.

For the past two weeks they had driven up and down the Gaza Strip. They had walked door to door, talked to motel employees, fast-food workers, people at the garages, the used-car dealerships, the small loan offices. Nobody knew anything, nobody had seen anything, nobody had heard anything. It wasn't until the report had come in on the dead woman's fingerprints and dental records that they were able to identify her.

Her name was Linda Sutton. Twenty-one years old, she had had a long history of Chicago prostitution arrests under a lot of different names, usually around Wrigley Field, nearly thirty miles from where her body had been found. The detectives had pulled her rap sheet and mug shots, and now they just had to verify that the person calling herself Linda Sutton was, in fact, Linda Sutton.

The mother let them in quietly. Her daughter had been missing for weeks now, and the presence of two plainclothes cops in her living room was enough to confirm her fears. Sam explained why they were there and then showed her the mug shot photos.

"Oh, God!" She put her hands to her face, as if to block out the sight.

"It's her?" Wilkosz asked softly.

"Yes," she said. "That's her, that's my Linda."

"When did you last see her?" Sam asked.

"Memorial Day weekend," the mother answered. Her voice was mechanical. "May 24 it was. Our whole family got together. You know, to celebrate the holiday and all. Linda brought her kids."

"Kids?"

"She's got an eight-year-old daughter and a little boy, just fifteen months old. My God, what's going to happen to them now?"

The mother said that she knew Linda had worked as a prostitute.

"Under different names?" Wilkosz asked.

"Yes," she said. "Lots of them, I guess."

And then, "I think I always knew something awful was going to happen to my Linda. I been trying my best to get her off the street for a long time now. I found her a job at the factory. A good job, nice hours, not too hard. I rented a small apartment for her over on West Madison Street. I thought, you know, with a new job and a decent place to live But Linda, she would miss work all the time, just not show up, and she would disappear for days at a time."

The detectives talked with Linda Sutton's brother and sister. They, too, had been with her at the Memorial Day family party, but they had nothing new to offer. The holiday had been the last time they'd seen their sister.

When they talked with Linda's boyfriend of three weeks, *Luke Biggers, he told them that he had been at the family party, too. Biggers, a sometimes janitor/painter, was obviously shaken by the news of Linda's death. He spoke slowly and tearfully.

"That night was the last time I saw her," he said. "Me and Linda left her mother's place and we were walking toward her new place on Madison. But when we got to the corner, Linda said she was going to see someone about getting some syrup. We had

---

*Names preceded by asterisks are fictitious throughout.

a fight about it. I hated her using that shit. We started to argue about it, but I knew it wasn't no use. She was going to do what she was going to do. I just walked away and left her there. I never saw her again."

The detectives knew what Biggers meant when he talked about syrup. Prescription cough syrup with codeine was a popular commodity on the West Side. It was the drug of choice for many young street women who craved a "high" but who were too scared of heroin or crack cocaine. Syrup was cheap and easy to get from any number of street-front, low-rent doctors not overly conscientious about their Hippocratic oath. Drinking a whole bottle of syrup would produce a dreamy, floating high that lasted for hours.

Wilkosz and Sam asked Luke Biggers if he would be willing to submit to a polygraph exam, and he readily agreed. They drove him to the county sheriff's office in Maywood, where he easily passed the test as to having no knowledge or participation in the murder of Linda Sutton.

Wilkosz left the next day for his annual vacation with his wife, getting as far away from the city as he could afford to go. Like most veteran police officers, he looked forward to these few weeks every year when he could escape the seamy underbelly of human and urban decay. Few big city police officers take their vacations in another big city, and in fact the little towns along the Illinois-Wisconsin border are dotted with hundreds of cabins and mobile homes belonging to Chicago-area police officers.

When he returned from vacation, Wilkosz found on his desk the coroner's report on Linda Sutton. He read it immediately, hoping for some clue to jump out at him that would give him a lead to follow. During his time off, two younger DuPage detectives had continued to pound the pavement along the Gaza Strip, and to talk further to the friends and family of Linda Sutton. But by now, even though murder cases are never officially closed, everybody in the office was convinced that, barring the sudden appearance of an informant or other minor miracle, this one was going to prove to be unsolvable. Wilkosz not only didn't care for that verdict, he hated it. He and John Sam would stay with the case, period.

"Damn," he said, leafing through the pages of the report again, wondering if he'd misread it. According to the coroner, Linda Sutton had not been dead for months, or even weeks, as he and Sam had surmised. She had been dead, according to this, just three days before her body was found.

"No, no, this can't be," Wilkosz said, reaching for the telephone. "Something's wrong here. Maybe the stenographer made a mistake or something."

"She was dead only three days?" he asked the coroner. "That can't be right."

"It is right," the coroner said. "The reason you guys were so off with your estimate is that the body received an immediate internal invasion of parasites, causing the unusual rapidity in the breakdown of the body tissue."

"In English, please, doc. What happened?"

"Ordinarily, invading parasites will first attack those portions of the body through which they can most quickly make internal entry, such as the eyes, the ear canals, the rectum. All that takes time—for the initial entry to be made, the larvae to develop and hatch. But in this case they didn't have to "force entry," if you will. Entry had already been made, through massive wounds in her chest."

"Wounds? What kind of wounds?"

"Well, to put it quite simply, if rather crudely, her breasts had been cut off."

Chapter Three

October 5, 1982

It was two o'clock in the morning. *Denise Gardner, a black prostitute, walked slowly along the sidewalk. She'd been working her usual corner, North Avenue and Throop in Chicago, near the huge Proctor and Gamble factory, but it had been a slow night, and she needed to score. Now she glanced behind her from time to time, staring boldly into the faces of passing drivers. It was a signal, a way to let them know that she was working. Just as taxicabs use a roof light to advertise their availability, and ice-cream vendors have their musical bells, street prostitutes radiate a smoky look and a butt-strut walk to say, "Here's something for sale."

Denise watched as a red van came to a stop at the intersection and then swung slowly around toward her. Sometimes the

33

cars slowed down, their drivers gawking at the passing parade of street love on display. Denise could usually spot which ones were just grabbing a free look and which ones might, with a little encouragement, become customers. It was a talent you learned out on the street. And the guy in this van, she could tell, was a pretty good "possible."

The van pulled over to the curb right next to her. Bold, this one, she thought, no circling the block five times to make sure, as some of them did when they couldn't admit to themselves what they were after, wanting to convince themselves instead that the prostitute had coaxed them into it. This is a man who knows what he's here for, Denise thought, and she walked up to the passenger side of the van.

The driver was a skinny white guy, about twenty-five or thirty years old. He smiled and looked her over, but didn't say anything.

"Looking for a date?" she asked.

Now he leaned across the passenger seat and lowered the window.

"How much?"

He had greasy-looking mouse brown hair, a wispy mustache, and big blue eyes. There was a kind of hillbilly look about him. But, Denise thought, he looked harmless enough, kind of stray-dog puppyish and underfed. And anyway, a score was a score.

Denise was calculating price even as she sized him up. The going rates for a street prostitute's services fluctuate with supply and demand. And for specialty services the price automatically skyrockets, not so much because of any reticence on the hooker's part as because she knows the market will bear it. "If you wanna play something special, you gotta pay something special" goes the saying on the street.

"Twenty bucks," Denise said.

"I'll give you twenty-five," he said, opening the passenger door and motioning her in.

Later, Denise would reflect that his offering more than she asked for should have tipped her off.

He seemed a little sweaty, a little nervous as he pulled out into traffic, but that was nothing unusual. Nearly all of these guys were married, and just because they were willing to go out and pay for what they wanted didn't mean they weren't nervous about getting caught. Some, too, went to hookers because they weren't functioning well with their usual partners, and they wanted to test out with a stranger whether the problem was theirs or the partner's.

As he drove, Denise checked him out. He wore a multicolored flannel shirt, blue jeans, and black, square-toed boots with stitching around the toes and zippers on the sides. Nothing special, nothing alarming.

At Willow and Burling, a quiet intersection with little traffic in a neighborhood of small factories, the man pulled over.

"Let's get comfortable," he said, "in the back."

"Sure, honey," Denise said. "Let's do that."

He opened a little door in a plywood partition leading to the back of the van, and motioned her through. The place smelled like a workshop, and she could see that the shelves that ran along the sides of the van in back were filled with tools, paint cans, nails, brushes, and other equipment.

"What are you, a carpenter?" she asked.

She turned around to face him. He was reaching up onto one of the shelves. When his hand came down, it held a gun.

"Oh, shit," Denise said, her heart suddenly galloping. Be cool, girl, she told herself, just be cool.

The man put the gun in her face, pushing its cold barrel against the center of her forehead.

"Just do everything I tell you," he said quietly, "and you won't get hurt."

Now she felt sweat pouring from her body. She had never even imagined such fear. "No problem, honey," she said, her voice coming out in a croak. "Really, you're the boss, honey. There ain't no problem here at all."

Carefully, she lifted her hands and showed her palms. It was instinctive, submissive, an offer of the least possible resistance.

Denise had been working the streets for years, and she had heard all the stories about "hooker freaks." The word *hooker* itself came into being during the Civil War because of Union General Joseph Hooker's fondness for ladies of pleasure. While the Army of the Potomac was camped outside Fredericksburg, Virginia, Hooker often sent an orderly into town to bring several women out to spend the night with him. When the women were challenged as they approached the camp sentries, the general's orderlies would call out: "Let them pass! They're Hooker's!"

Almost every street prostitute had a "hooker freak" story to tell. Some freaks were harmless; they wanted to get laid in a coffin or wear the hooker's underwear on their head while she screamed filthy words at them. Or they asked her to urinate on them, or scold them for being naughty boys. They were the pitiful ones and the hookers laughed about them, and charged them enormous sums for the privilege of being humiliated.

But then, there was the other kind of

freak. Guys with guns. Guys with razors. Guys with matches. Guys who got harder the louder they made you scream. If there was one thing a street prostitute feared more than cops, more than an angry pimp, more than hunger or cold or disease, it was the sadistic hooker freak.

Denise had never run into a freak before, but she knew what all the girls said to do: keep your cool, don't rattle his chain.

For a long time the man stared at her, as if he was deciding exactly what his next move was. Denise couldn't tell if he'd been doing drugs or was just a psycho, but it didn't really matter. Either way she knew she was in trouble.

Finally he spoke. "Take off your clothes," he said.

"Fine, honey, just fine. Whatever you say."

Quickly she stripped off her clothes and dropped them to the floor of the van. The walls of the small truck seemed to close in on her. She felt as if she were in a cage.

When she was naked, he waved the gun in her face. "On your knees," he ordered.

Denise did as she was told. The man stepped behind her. God, he's going to shoot me in the back of the head, she thought. There was a terrible moment of panic while she closed her eyes and waited for the explosion. She tensed her leg muscles, wanting to jump up and run out screaming into the night, but too paralyzed by fear even to move.

Click.

It wasn't the click of a gun. It was hand-cuffs. He snapped one cuff on, then pulled back her other arm and cuffed it. Having her hands bound behind her made her feel more vulnerable than just being naked ever had. The entire front of her body felt like a target.

He came around to the front of her. Denise bent her head down, said nothing. She just wanted to get through this, whatever this was going to be, without setting the freak off. She kept telling herself that a lot of guys liked to bind a girl's hands as part of their sex play, but they usually didn't hurt her. Maybe, please God, that's all this was.

Denise heard him rummaging in the shelves again. What could he be looking for? Suddenly he was in her face again, this time wielding a butcher knife. The blade, gleaming and sharp, seemed to be a foot long.

He opened his pants. "Do it," he said, "or I use the knife."

She did as she was told, nearly choking from the violence of his thrusts. When it was over, he backed away and went up to the front of the van. Denise's arms ached from being pinned behind her, and she was numb with fear. But she had found that men could change drastically after orgasm, and she hoped now that he'd had his fun he would let her go. Maybe he was getting ready to drive someplace where he would then just push her out.

But he did not get behind the wheel. He dug around in the cab of the van and then came back with a can of Coke. And something else in his hands. He stepped behind her and clamped another cuff on her arm. Then he yanked her close to the side of the truck. He snapped the other cuff around a support brace. Denise heard a car pass them. She wanted to scream for help, but she knew she would not be heard, and he might slit her throat before she could even try.

He stood in front of her, holding the Coke in one hand. He held out his other hand. There were pills in it, about fifteen of them, aqua blue capsules. Denise knew about many kinds of pills, but she didn't recognize these.

"Swallow these," he ordered. "All of them."

He forced the capsules into her mouth. She tried to use her tongue to push them up against her gums, but he forced her head back and poured the Coke down her throat until she had to swallow all of them.

Then, in the dim yellow light of the van, she saw him go back to his shelves. Things were getting hazy now. She couldn't think straight. He came back with something in his hands. It was long. Yellow and white. A cord. What, she thought, what is this? She was fading away, a loud rushing noise in her ears, her eyes slipping out of focus.

She was still half conscious when he pushed her down on the floor and climbed on top of her. I'm dying, she thought vaguely, I will never wake up from this night.

Before she passed out, her last thought was that something even more terrible was about to happen to her.

Chapter Four

The day dawned clear and bright in Chicago. By late morning the temperature had risen into the high fifties, and the air was crisp, the sun brilliant. Red and gold leaves swirled in eddies along the streets and Halloween decorations were going up in neighborhood storefronts. This was the kind of day that inspires songs about the glories of autumn. But for *Fred Smithson, age seventy-two, it was not a day for singing.

Just after dawn, Smithson made his way slowly down an alley in the 2700 block of North Maplewood, as he did every morning. Smithson knew the Sanitation Department's schedule better than its drivers did, and he carefully planned his route to get to the full trash dumpsters blocks ahead of them. Now, dragging his plastic trash bag, he peered into garbage cans and sifted through mounds of rubbish. If he could find enough beer and soda cans and bits of aluminum foil, he could trade them for a few dollars, and he would be able to buy food today. If not, he would eat Alpo.

The early morning chill caused the old man's arthritis to act up. He stopped every few minutes to blow on his hands and rub his swollen red knuckles. His fingerless woolen gloves helped ward off some of the chill, but not enough to ease the ache that was always with him.

When Smithson got halfway down the alley, he stopped again. He held his hands to his mouth to warm them, and stared at what seemed to be yet another pile of trash in the overflowing alley. But as he focused more carefully, he realized that the pile of trash had blood leaking from it. His empty stomach churned as he shuffled closer and peered down for a closer inspection.

A young black woman lay naked in the alley. Facedown. Still. "Lord have mercy on us all!" he cried. "It's a body, a dead body!" He hobbled to the end of the alley, shouting for help.

Windows began opening in the surrounding factories, and faces peeked out as people heard the old man's cries.

In minutes Chicago Fire Department paramedics pulled into the alley in their red and white mobile emergency unit. Uniformed patrolmen blocked off both ends of the alley, the squad cars' blue bubble lights revolving. The factory workers had gathered in the alley to see what kind of violence had happened. They stepped back to make room for the paramedics, who knelt down on either side of the woman. "She's dead," said one of the onlookers in a hushed voice. "Maybe not," said another. "You notice the blood's still fresh."

The paramedics carefully turned her over.

The woman was gray faced and unconscious, but her heart was still beating. She was alive.

Her left breast had been crudely removed, and the white glint of rib bones was visible through the ragged hole in her chest. Her right breast lay alongside her arm, attached to her body only by shreds of tissue. Several people in the alley put their hands over their mouths and turned away.

The paramedics did what they could to stanch the flow of blood and then started an immediate IV glucose drip, to counteract massive shock. They lifted her onto a stretcher and put her in the ambulance. By the time they reached the mouth of the alley, where the squad car backed up to let them out, they were on a mobile telephone with Illinois Masonic Hospital, alerting the emergency room to put a trauma team together.

At the hospital, the woman was rushed into an emergency room cubicle. Blood oozed from the thick swaddle of bandages on her chest. When the trauma team had packed the wound and stanched the flow of blood, Dr. Steven Kavka, the hospital's plastic surgeon, came in. He started procedures to graft skin from the woman's thigh, to be used later in repairing the remaining breast. But there was little more he could do until her vital signs were stabilized.

By evening the police knew who she was. Denise Gardner. When detectives arrived at the hospital, the doctor in charge told them that her condition had been upgraded from critical to extremely serious, and they would be allowed to speak to her. "But keep it short," he said. "And I mean that. She's in very bad shape, so don't push it."

Denise lay motionless in the dim room, the only sound the steady ping of the heart monitor. Her vision was blurry, everything out of focus, but she could sense chrome and dozens of small blinking lights that cast a red glow over the white sheet that covered her. She knew she was in a hospital. She knew she was still alive. On either side of her bed were metal stands. They held drooping plastic bags, with tubes that led into her arms. Next to her bed was a stainless-steel machine that fed a plastic tube into her mouth.

It whooshed out tiny puffs of air in a steady beat.

"Denise?" she heard.

She blinked, tried to see things more clearly. It was a man. Two men, standing by her bed. Plainclothes cops. She wasn't so far gone that she didn't know cops. Detectives, they must be. Narcs and vice guys dress grubby. Detectives wear suits.

"We're Chicago detectives," one of the men said. He told her the names, but she couldn't understand. "We're here to find out what happened to you. Do you understand?"

She tried to speak, but no sounds came out. It was as if her vocal cords were not connected to her brain. Finally, she could only cough and nod her head.

"We know you can't talk," the older detective said. He seemed nice, as though he felt bad that they were bothering her. "We just have some questions. We'll try to make them yes or no questions. You blink if it's yes, shake your head if it's no, okay?"

Denise blinked.

It seemed to take forever, but she was able to answer most of the questions.

"Blink if he was white, shake your head if he was black," the detective said. Denise blinked.

"Blink when I say the color of his hair. Black? Blond? Brown?" Denise blinked.

He handed her a pad of paper and a pen. She was able to scrawl "mustache" and "blue jeans" and "flannel shirt" and "greasy hair."

When she had managed to describe the man, including the black square-toed boots with the zippers on the side and the stitching around the toes, they asked her about the offender's car. Again, it was slow and painful, but it made her feel alive to be doing something. Her body was numb and she didn't yet know everything that had happened to her. She only knew that her chest hurt very badly, the doctor had said something about her breasts having been cut, and she wanted the cops to catch that sick son of a bitch.

With her scrawled notes and labored signals, she was able to tell the detectives that it had been a red van, that it was clean and new looking with dark-tinted windows, and there was a little wooden door that separated the front from the back.

When she had used up the little strength she had, the detectives said they would go. They looked down at her sympathetically. "Hang in there," one of them said. She could see from the look in his eyes that he was not sure she would make it.

"We'll let you rest now," the other detective

said. "But we'll need to talk to you again soon."

She nodded. The detectives began to walk out. Suddenly Denise remembered something. She wanted to tell them. They were going through the door. She threw her arm out hard against the metal stanchion beside her to get their attention. The stanchion rattled and they turned. Denise signaled them to come back.

"What is it?"

She signaled for the notebook. The detective handed it to her, and she scrawled the words "roach clip," "rearview mirror," "2 feathers," "white," "blue."

Chapter Five

"Bright red," Detective Phil Murphy said. "Tinted windows. Could it be?"

It was a cool October evening and Murphy, along with his partner, Chicago Area Five Detective Tom Flynn, was on his way to a routine witness-statement call. But now, in the 2500 block of North Central Avenue, Murphy saw the van, and it fit the description that had gone out after the interview with Denise Gardner.

For two weeks Chicago police officers had been pulling over red vans, orange vans, pink, copper, and maroon vans. There had been many false alarms, some irate citizens who'd been stopped more than once, but the only break in the Gardner case had been a bad break. Area Five detectives had learned, from the factory's security director, that the Proctor and Gamble plant in front of which

Denise Gardner had met her attacker had a roving security camera in operation that night. Detectives from Area Five had gone to the factory and sat in the security office, watching the grainy black-and-white tape over and over, hoping to get lucky. And they almost did.

At 4:52:26 A.M., the tape showed two female black women strolling slowly along North Avenue. The taller of the two, wearing a light-colored blouse, was thought to be the girl Denise had been working with that night. The other, shorter girl resembled Denise herself.

At 4:54:47, the taller girl could be seen walking toward a car that had pulled to the curb. Six seconds later, a dark van pulled to the curb and the shorter girl walked toward it. At that very instant the camera automatically switched views to another area of the plant.

The detectives borrowed the security tape and took it to a film-processing lab, where they had each frame in that six-second interval enlarged and freeze-framed. But just as the van pulled to the curb, the driver touched the brakes and the resultant halo effect of bright brake lights in the dark obscured the rear license plate. The film processor tried enlarging just that section, darkening it and lightening the contrast, but nothing worked. No matter what they did they could not get a look at the van's license plate.

Slipping through traffic now, Murphy and Flynn took note of the license plate on the van in front of them. Then Flynn swung into the left lane so they were driving alongside the van. Murphy glanced over.

"Well, what do you know!" Murphy said. "Looks like a plywood partition behind the driver, just like Gardner said."

Murphy also saw that there was something hanging from the rearview mirror.

"Correct me if I'm wrong here," he said, "but is that, or is it not, a roach clip with two long feathers? And if I'm not colorblind, which I'm not, one of those feathers is blue and one of those feathers is white."

Murphy reached for the radio and called in the location and the van's license number, telling the police dispatcher they were getting ready to pull the vehicle over. Flynn tapped a quick blast on the squad car's siren and flashed the spotlight into the driver's mirror. The van pulled to the curb.

Murphy and Flynn climbed out of their squad car, unsnapping their holsters and moving cautiously. Murphy kept an eye on the driver while Flynn watched the passenger side and the little door that hid the rear compartment of the van.

"Police officers," Murphy said. "Roll down the window."

The driver rolled the window down, and both detectives took a good look at him. He was young, white, about average height and build. He wore a white T-shirt and jeans. But his hair was not mouse brown and greasy, the way Denise had described her attacker's hair. This guy's hair was a big red fuzzy bush. Murphy was immediately reminded of Bozo the Clown.

The detectives noted that the driver had orange eyebrows, too, over small, close-set blue eyes. By now Flynn had checked out the rear compartment of the van. Nobody was there. Flynn came around to the front, glanced at the driver, then shook his head at his partner. The two detectives were sure that this was not the man who had mutilated Denise Gardner. But they were just as sure that this *was* the van.

"Step out of the van," Murphy said. "Keep your hands out in front of you where I can see them."

The young van driver looked frightened. He started to stutter something, then stopped. He climbed out of the van, making a big show of keeping his hands high in the air.

"What's your name?" Murphy asked.

"Eddie Spreitzer," he said, jumping at the sound of Murphy's voice.

"How old are you, Eddie?"

"Twenty-one, sir," he said. "But I didn't do nothing," he nearly shouted.

Though Spreitzer was answering their questions, the detectives found him hard to understand. Spreitzer spoke poorly through his thick lips, in broken sentences and jumbled syntax.

"This your van, Eddie?"

"Oh, no, it ain't mine." Eddie seemed inordinately glad of that fact. "It belongs to my boss."

"Uh-huh. Who's your boss, Eddie, and where is he?"

"His name's Robin, Robin Gecht." Eddie waved his arm in a northward direction. "He's over at this place where he's fixin' it, I mean, we're both fixin' it. Remodeling a place, a basement, and all that."

"Where?"

"It's 3042 North Linder. It's just up that way, over there, I mean. A few blocks, you know, and over."

The two detectives looked at each other, sharing the same thought. This kid talked as though he had a mouth full of marbles.

"Well, I tell you what, Eddie. We want to talk to your boss, you know what I mean? So you're going to get back in your van and

drive real nice and slow to that address on
Linder. And we're going to get back in our
squad car and follow you there. All that okay
with you, Eddie?"

"Uh, sure. I mean, yeah, okay. Sure.
Whatever." Eddie Spreitzer, sweating heavily
now, clambered back into the van.

They drove north on Central and then east
a block, pulling up in front of the Linder address. It was an old raised, bay-fronted brick
house of the type called a Queen Anne, and
it sat square and solid in the midst of thousands of other homes just like it. This was
one of Chicago's two vast "bungalow belts."
This Northwest neighborhood and Chicago's
equally sprawling Southwest side comprised
many miles of brown, red, or yellow brick
homes on small plots. Graced with the ma-
turity of half-century-old oak and maple
trees that often overhung the street, most of
these residences had been built as WPA
projects during the Depression.

Eddie Spreitzer pulled the van up in front
of the job site, and the detectives slid their
squad car to the curb behind him. Eddie
jumped out and started walking, fast,
toward the house.

"Oh, no, Eddie, uh-uh," Murphy said.
"You stay right here with us. Just call out.
Tell him to come out here."

Eddie stopped in his tracks, looking wild-eyed. The two detectives looked at each other and shrugged. Was it them he was so afraid of? Or was it his boss? And if so, why?

"Robin! Robin, come on out here," Spreitzer called. "Some guys here, they want to talk to you." Eddie turned to the detectives with a quick smile, seeking approval. But then, the smile gone as quick as it came, he turned back. "But I didn't do nothing wrong," he called out toward the house.

He came out through the side door and walked toward them. He was about five seven, 130 pounds. He had greasy-looking mouse brown hair, a wispy mustache, and piercing pale blue eyes. He was wearing a plaid work shirt, jeans, and black boots with square, stitched toes and zippers on the sides.

"Bingo," Murphy said softly.

"What seems to be the problem?" the man asked, looking from one detective to another.

"Your van."

"My van? What about it?" His attitude bespoke friendliness, courtesy, and only the mildest curiosity.

"It looks like one that was used in a recent crime. In fact, it looks an *awful* lot like it. Isn't that something?"

The detectives deliberately kept the details vague, watching for a reaction. But clearly,

Robin Gecht was a much cooler customer than his friend Eddie Spreitzer.

"Wow," he said, "isn't that something? Must be a real coincidence, huh?"

Two other men came out of the house, and walked toward them.

"This is my brother, Everett, and my brother-in-law, Tom," Gecht said easily, as if he were introducing his family to old friends.

Both detectives nodded to the newcomers. "You guys ever use this van?"

Gecht answered for them. "We're the only ones who ever drive it," he said, motioning around to the little group. "And Rosemary, of course."

"Rosemary?"

"My wife."

As the detectives asked innocuous questions of the men—where they lived, with whom, what their ages were, they kept a sharp eye on the unspoken dynamics of the group. Gecht's brother and brother-in-law crowded forward, answering without hesitation, obviously wanting to know what all the excitement was about and eager to be a part of it. Eddie Spreitzer, on the other hand, hung back half behind his boss. He rolled his eyes, he chewed on his knuckles, he stood on one foot and then the other, and he bit his bottom lip. His forehead was beaded with sweat on this cool autumn evening, and his eyes whipped back and forth between the detectives and his boss.

"Sometimes," Murphy later recalled, "you can learn a lot more with your eyes than with your ears. People will say what they feel they need to say in a given situation, for whatever their reasons might be. But their body language will have a whole lot of truth to tell you about what's really going on inside their heads. You didn't have to be a psychiatrist to know that Eddie Spreitzer was almost goofy with fear, and that it was Robin Gecht he was afraid of."

Gecht himself stood smiling and at ease, making no overt gesture that would indicate fear or emotional turmoil. In fact, thought the detectives, he was behaving altogether too nonchalant for somebody whose driver had been followed by plainclothes detectives because his van resembled the vehicle used in a crime. Gecht didn't ask what kind of crime his van was implicated in, and he was pointedly ignoring the fact that his helper, Eddie Spreitzer, was jiggling around like a marionette on strings. Gecht's playacting was good, Murphy decided. Too good to be true.

Finally, the detectives asked if all four men would accompany them back to Area Five, only a few blocks away, so the matter of the "coincidence" of the red van could be cleared up.

Gecht answered for all of them. "Certainly," he said, "we want to cooperate fully." He turned to the other two men, who also nodded. Eddie Spreitzer looked long and meaningfully at his boss, as though trying to convey a message without words. "Right, Eddie?" Gecht asked. "We want to cooperate with these detectives, right?"

Spreitzer looked from Murphy and Flynn to Gecht and back again. "Uh, sure, right. We want to cooperate."

The detectives put Robin Gecht in the back of their squad car. The others were allowed to drive the van back to the station. Murphy and Flynn tailgated the van all the way into the Area Five parking lot. Inside, they took their quartet up to the second-floor detective squad room.

"We told our commander, Lieutenant John Minogue, who we'd brought in and why," Murphy said. "Minogue's not the type to interfere or try to micro-manage his detectives. He told us to stay with the case. He would keep an eye on the operation, just to be sure that everything was done by the book and would stand up in court later."

By now word was spreading throughout the large squad room that Murphy and Flynn had brought in a good "possible" in the hooker-slasher case. Detectives wandered by, peering through the long, narrow glass panel at the side of the interrogation room door. Several whistled and gave a thumbs-up sign as they walked away from the door behind which Robin Gecht sat. This was a case in which the witness description, which they all knew by heart, matched perfectly with the suspect, something that almost never happens.

Several detectives made it a point to stroll casually by the desk where Flynn and Murphy were putting their case file together.

"Nice stop," said one.

"Good pinch," said another. Flynn and Murphy nodded their thank-yous for the understated salutes. What none of them could know at the time is that the "nice stop" of the red van would turn out to be the stop of the decade.

Chapter Six

It was later that afternoon when Murphy and Flynn returned to Denise Gardner's hospital room. Denise sat in a wheelchair, with a food tray resting on the arms of the chair. It had been two weeks since the attack, but she still looked dangerously gaunt.

"We want you to look at some photos," Murphy said. "Tell us if one of them is the man who hurt you." He and Flynn had taken Polaroids of Gecht and his helpers, and then added a couple photos of other men to the stack. The men were all white, all somewhat similar in appearance. But Denise did not hesitate. "He's there," she said. "Monster who cut me up is right there."

"Which?" Flynn asked.

"Him," she said, jabbing the photo of Robin Gecht. "It's him, all right. He's even wearing the same shirt!"

"Because Denise had identified Robin from a set of photos," Murphy says, "we still had to follow up with a live lineup. And because our victim obviously couldn't come to the lineup, we were going to have to bring the lineup to her, in the hospital."

While that might seem to be a simple enough process, it's not. When the priorities of the police and a hospital cross, there are always delicate negotiations. To the hospital everything, rightfully, must take second place to the well-being of the patient. To the police, everything else is secondary to the apprehension of the criminal.

While it may seem at times that the police are unmindful of a victim's pain, they will tell you that the victim's pain is one of the things that drives them relentlessly to pursue a case.

"But we have to have the facts quickly," Murphy said, "despite the victim's pain. A year after the crime a victim's pain will be healed, but whether or not the person who caused it is behind bars depends largely on what we can gather immediately."

What Murphy says is confirmed by many studies that have shown that every day that passes between the commission of a crime and the involvement of the police reduces the chance of it being solved. Victims die, they change their minds, they move away or even lose interest.

Though suspects would ordinarily stand in

a lineup, it was decided that because Denise would be viewing it from a wheelchair, the men would instead sit in order to be at eye level with the witness. Murphy could see that it was a moment Denise dreaded.

The detectives watched carefully as she was rolled into the hospital corridor just outside her room. Folding chairs had been placed in a line. The lineup consisted of Robin, Eddie, Tom, Everett, and two other similarly built men, all of whom had been brought over from Area Five in separate detective cars. Suspects are immediately separated in this way so that they can't concoct stories together, and no one of them will have any way of knowing what the others are telling the police.

Illinois law provides that for each suspect in a lineup, two other similar persons be provided. Robin Gecht was the primary suspect, of course, but the detectives didn't know yet what Eddie Spreitzer's role was. Two suspects; six men.

Denise moved slowly forward, her tubes trailing behind her. She was still breathing through one of them. She looked at the six men, and her face went still. Murphy could see that she was reliving the panic of that night. For a few seconds he was afraid that she would back away from this, just turn back and not face the man who had hurt her. But suddenly Denise started shrieking and pointing.

"It's him! That's the guy! That's the one right there!"

She pointed directly at Robin Gecht. Through the rubber tube in her mouth, she began to make whistling, wheezing noises. "That's the bastard!" she cried. Then she pitched forward and crashed to the floor. All the stainless steel tripods with their dripping, connected plastic bags crashed around her. Nurses, who had been standing off to the side, rushed in to help her. And then she passed out.

Murphy and Flynn stepped forward. They had gone by the book, and they had gotten results. "Robin Gecht, you're under arrest for the attempted murder of Denise Gardner," Murphy intoned. "You have the right to remain silent . . ."

Gecht, with an open-mouthed expression, put his hand to his chest in the classic "Who, me?" pose. But the detectives could see rage, and the first glitter of fear, in his eyes. The actor was still acting, but the role he was playing had just become a lot more difficult.

When Flynn and Murphy got back to Area Five, Gecht's wife, Rosemary, was waiting. She was, Murphy thought, bizarre looking, with long black hair, Cleopatra eye makeup, long red fingernails, and a hard-eyed stare. Eventually some of the detectives would come to believe that Rosemary deliberately tried to cultivate a "witch-lady" image.

"She would lean forward and stare," one detective says, "never blinking, widening those eyes at you like she thought she was putting a spell on you or something. But it came across silly, like a TV show."

Murphy and Flynn sat down with Rosemary and tried to discuss Robin's whereabouts on the night of October 5.

"Could you tell us where he was?" they asked.

Rosemary's responses were terse and hostile.

"He was home that night," she said.

"All night?"

"Yes, all night. He never left the house. I'll swear to it."

"Does he ever go out at night?"

"Sometimes."

"Well, how could you possibly remember *that* night as opposed to any other?"

Rosemary suddenly stood and snatched up her purse.

"I'm not saying anything else until I talk to a lawyer." She turned and stalked out of the room.

Later that night Robin Gecht was formally charged with the attack on Denise Gardner.

The charges were aggravated battery, deviate sexual assault, armed robbery, and kidnapping. He was taken downstairs to the lockup to be fingerprinted and photographed, and then, after his prints cleared, he was taken to Cook County Jail at 26th and California, where his bond was set at $50,000.

The turn-of-the-century Jail and Criminal Courts Building was a massive granite structure surrounded by towering barbed-wire fences and bristling with guards, metal detectors, and automated alarm systems. It was commonly known to police officers as "26th and Cal." Among themselves, its unwilling tenants called it the "Graystone Hotel."

Detective Tom Flynn drove to 26th and Cal the next morning to see if Gecht was ready to make a statement. He could have saved the trip.

"I have nothing to say to you," Gecht said, his mouth tight, his eyes like steel. "Talk to my lawyer."

Chapter Seven

October 20, 1982

When Warren Wilkosz arrived at his office at the DuPage County Sheriff's office, he was told that he'd gotten a call from Mike Herigodt in Area Five.

"Herigodt? Oh, sure, I talked to him last year after the Sutton murder."

"Well, maybe something's come up. Herigodt said he wanted to let you know about a prostitute being attacked in Chicago."

A prostitute, Wilkosz thought. Could it possibly be a break in the Linda Sutton case after all this time? The picture of that dead girl stretched out in the grass, her hands cuffed behind her back, had never left his mind. Sutton might have been a hooker, but that didn't matter. To Wilkosz, to most homicide detectives, a murdered bag lady or wino or dope addict has as much right to justice as anyone else. "That," he says, "is because for those of us who have made a career of catching murderers, it is the killer who absorbs all our focus rather than the victim."

As he dialed Herigodt's number, he prayed for a break. But when he got through to Area Five, Herigodt was out. Wilkosz hung up, frustrated. Prostitute, he thought. What could it be other than some connection with the Linda Sutton case that would prompt Chicago's Area Five to get on the phone to him out in suburban DePage County?

Wilkosz had done a lot of thinking about prostitutes since that day behind the Moonlit Motel. The girls, he had found, were an odd breed. Each had her own story, her own reason for choosing an ugly, humiliating, and dangerous line of work. Many of the ones he had met bore knife-wound scars on their faces, missing fingers, broken teeth, and unset bone fractures.

Though they seemed in many ways to be loners, the "working girls" were almost obsessively interested in one another's doings. They kept track of each other's births, deaths, triumphs, tricks, and close calls. When they were locked up, usually once or twice a week for the regulars, they couldn't wait to get through processing so they could get together in the "bullpen." There they liked to sleep, not on the steel benches, but under them, on the floor, where four, five, or six girls would curl up and wind around each other for warmth and security. Street hookers, Wilkosz had found, will share with each other every (often grossly exaggerated) detail of the sick tricks out there; who to watch out for, which vehicle to avoid; what to do or not to do if you met up with a particular type of sick date.

And yet, despite the camaraderie among them, they regularly snitched to the police at the lockup that one of the girls "has a hypo stashed up her bootie" or another is "wanted in Area Two for trick-robbin." These unsolicited admissions were invariably followed by: "Can you get me out quicker now?" or "Can I have an extra baloney sandwich?" Even while they clung together, they would turn on one another as quick as an eyeblink. It was a slippery, treacherous way of life, but it was all of life they knew.

Hooker murders weren't news to either Warren Wilkosz in suburban DuPage County or to Chicago's Area Five detectives. The lives of the working girls tended to be rough, cheap, and short. Whatever life on the street, the brutality of their pimps, or constant degradation didn't accomplish, drugs and disease usually did.

But Linda Sutton had not died from drugs or disease. She had been murdered, and Wilkosz believed his job was to find her killer and bring him in. That he had been unable to solve his case for a year and a half grated at him.

The telephone rang. It was Herigodt.

"Warren, you remember that Linda Sutton murder, year and a half ago? The hooker you guys found out there with her breasts cut up?"

"Yes, Mike, I remember," Wilkosz said drily.

"Well, we've got something up here that I think you're going to find mighty interesting."

"And that is . . . ?"

"A hooker, name of Denise Gardner, she's one of our regulars. A john picks her up in a red van. She gives him a price of twenty dollars, he says he'll go twenty-five. Tells you right there something's out of whack, don't it?"

"Either that," Wilkosz answered, "or the guy's a philanthropist, but I bet you're going to tell me that's not the case, right? What happened, Mike?"

"She gets in and he drives off a ways, over by some small side street with factories where nobody's around. Pulls out a gun. Turns out he's a hooker freak. And now here's the part that'll start your wheels turning. He cuffs her."

"You're serious. Handcuffs?" A picture of

Linda Sutton's nude, decomposed body, the cheap nickel-plated cuffs still attached to her wrists, flashed in Wilkosz's memory.

"You heard it right. Handcuffs. Then our guy proceeds to drug her, do his thing with her, and then he winds a cord around her breasts and cuts them off with a knife."

"Jesus, Mary, and Joseph," Wilkosz whispered.

"And here's the good news," Herigodt added. "She lived. She gave us a good description and we picked him up. Him, his red van, and his weird friends."

"I'm on the way," Wilkosz said, reaching forward to hang up the phone. "Oh, wait? Mike? What's this maniac's name?"

"His name's Robin Gecht."

"Well, Mr. Robin Gecht, here I come."

Chapter Eight

Chicago is geographically divided, for police purposes, into twenty-five districts. Four or five districts clumped together are called an area. Follow-up units such as detectives, youth officers, and gang-crimes specialists work area-wide. Area Five comprises the whole Northwest side of Chicago, and includes Districts 14, 15, 16, 17, and the newly created 25. Area Five headquarters is known as Grand Central Station, a name selected by schoolchildren in a contest because of its location at North Central and West Grand Avenue. It is a huge, spacious building that houses the 25th District police station and a modern detective headquarters, along with a youth division and gang-crimes section.

The new building replaced the old Shakespeare District (in Chicago, police districts are named after the street they're on, or the neighborhood they're in), which dated from

1883 and was a massive warren of steep, worn marble stairways, tiny, narrow rooms with tinier, narrower windows, and dank rows of forgotten horse stalls in the basement.

Grand Central, next door to two Cook County circuit court branches, opened with much fanfare in December 1981. Then-Mayor Jane Byrne, along with several city aldermen, local politicians, and a battalion of police brass, attended the opening cere-monies. Reporters duly noted the airy spa-ciousness of the glass and steel-beam construction, and the soft mauve and muted orange of the lockup areas, said by some behaviorists to instill a sense of calm and well-being. The new building also featured sophisticated internal cameras and alarm systems that would alert a desk sergeant if someone in the lockups or in a rear interro-gation room was in trouble. Like most mod-ern government buildings, Grand Central is huge, well lighted, efficiently designed, and utterly without character.

After his call from Detective Herigodt, War-ren Wilkosz drove into Chicago's Area Five to meet with detectives on the second floor of Grand Central. Yes, he could certainly talk to Gecht, they told him, but not yet. Chicago was still trying to talk to him, and no one wanted to break the flow. For now he could have Eddie Spreitzer. He met Spreitzer in Interrogation Room F.

"The guy looked like Howdy Doody," Wilkosz says. "His red hair stood up in all directions and he had clown lips. This was not a good-looking guy."

But the dominant impression Wilkosz had of Eddie Spreitzer was not his looks, it was his manner. Eddie was terrified. His face and shirtfront dripped with sour, acrid sweat from fear. He seemed to be panting rather than breathing. He wrung his hands and wiped his face and picked mindlessly and viciously at his protruding lower lip and at his fiercely bitten fingernails.

Why? Wilkosz asked himself. Something was very wrong here. Eddie was only in the police station because he'd been seen driving the van of a suspect. He wasn't accused of anything. Yet even when Wilkosz asked the most innocuous questions—where do you live, what do you do for a living—Eddie would jump.

There is a subtle art to interrogation, and good detectives learn to gear their style of questioning to the personality of the person being questioned. Tread softly if the person seems shy or reluctant to talk. Come on stronger if he's trying to play mind games. Bring out both barrels if he comes on macho and hostile. Wilkosz knew how to play these types, but Eddie Spreitzer was none of them.

"Eddie Spreitzer was dirty, pure and simple," says Wilkosz. "I knew it, Chicago knew it, and Eddie knew we knew it. Whatever his boss, Robin Gecht, was involved in, Eddie was involved in, too. He reeked of it. And it wasn't us that Eddie was so afraid of—it was Gecht. All I had to do was mention Gecht's name, and Eddie would jump like I'd jabbed him with a cattle prod. Every bone in my body told me this kid was dirty. It wasn't just a hunch, it was much more than that, right from the start. It's an accumulation of what you learn over the years of endless interrogations. You learn to read the body language, you listen as clearly to what is not said as to what is, you watch and listen and you watch some more. I knew that Robin was dirty, and I knew that Eddie was the kind who would eventually break. But not yet. I could see that Robin had some kind of hold on him. I couldn't break through it."

After he talked awhile with Eddie Spreitzer and got nowhere, Wilkosz sat quietly at one of the worktables in Area Five and waited for his chance at Robin Gecht. He'd waited more than a year and a half for something to break in the Linda Sutton case and this, he hoped, was the moment.

The similarities between the Sutton murder and the Denise Gardner attack were striking. Both women were black, both were Chicago prostitutes, both had been handcuffed, and both had had their breasts crudely hacked off. The main difference between the attacks was that Linda Sutton had died in a vacant suburban field, and Denise Gardner had lived to tell about it.

When one man kills a number of prostitutes, the obvious and immediate reference in the public's mind is to Jack the Ripper, and there is an assumption that such a man is driven by some "calling" or "divine mission" to rid the world of the painted strumpets of the night. But police knew better, just as the London police of the late 1800s knew better. Prostitutes are often chosen as murder victims simply because they are easy targets. They are transient, and, best of all, they will jump into a car with any stranger who flashes a $20 bill.

In the early 1980s, the concept of a random, repeat murderer who hunted and butchered human beings purely for the lust of the sport, and whose crime scenes were practically photocopies of each other, was just coming into being in police circles around the country. New terms had entered the language, experimented with and refined first among law enforcement officers, and then spreading to the public at large. Terms like *signature crimes, mass murderer, spree killer,* and *serial killer.*

In 1972, at the FBI Training Academy in Quantico, Virginia, some New York detectives started talking with some of their counterparts from New Orleans, and the men compared notes on several open cases from each jurisdiction. To everyone's surprise, they found that the crime scenes in New York matched nearly identically with those in New Orleans. Ergo, they were probably looking for the same man. The idea that specific conditions found at a crime scene could be used to identify a killer grew. Not only what the killer did, but why he did it just that way, and how his thought processes worked based on the evidence he left behind, became an important new tool for the police, a tool called *profiling.* The FBI now boasts a 65–70 percent accuracy rate in profiling a serial killer's personality type based on assessment of the crime scene alone.

So Wilkosz wondered, as did all the detectives working on the case, if they had a serial killer on their hands. The fact that Denise Gardner was alive instead of a homicide statistic was due to luck or perhaps to her young, strong constitution. But it was certainly not due to any less than deadly intent on Gecht's part. The detectives did not doubt that Gecht had assumed Denise Gardner was dying or already dead when he dumped her in the alley.

Wilkosz's meeting with Robin Gecht was not productive. Gecht was friendly, overly friendly, in fact, but he adamantly claimed he was innocent. Wilkosz showed him photos of Linda Sutton, and Gecht denied ever having seen her.

"I've never hurt anybody in my life," he said. "It's all a mistake."

Gecht was a slick talker. He had a way of opening his puppy dog eyes wide and blinking back tears that could fool a lot of people, but not a homicide cop, who has seen every Academy Award performance there is.

After several irritating hours of getting nowhere, Wilkosz gave up for the night and went home, angry and frustrated.

He had a lot to think about as he drove back to DuPage County. Denise Gardner had identified Robin Gecht as her attacker and, according to Denise, Gecht had been alone. So where did Eddie Spreitzer fit in? Could he have been there with Gecht during the Washington attack, hiding somewhere as a backup? Had Eddie, a year and a half ago out in DuPage County, been in unincorporated Villa Park? Had Eddie been there when Linda Sutton died?

Chapter Nine

November 5, 1982

It was a gray, wet noontime when Warren Wilkosz left the Carpentersville, Illinois, police station. The rain had started the night before, and weather reports promised no let-up all weekend. Wilkosz was almost to the tollway when his pocket pager started beeping. He glanced at the callback number, and was surprised to find that it belonged to the Carpentersville police chief. Wilkosz had just left his office. He turned off the highway and started looking for a gas station, so he could call in.

Wilkosz was in Carpentersville, a west suburban blue-collar town of thirty thousand, because that's where Robin Gecht and his wife and three kids were. Gecht had been out on bond in the Denise Gardner case for two weeks. To the surprise of the arresting detectives, *Bridget Ross, the middle-aged woman whose house Gecht had been remodeling, had put up his ten percent surety bond.

"Can you believe it?" Wilkosz says. "This woman mortgaged her home to come up with the money to bond Robin Gecht out of jail."

Soon after Gecht posted bail, he and his family moved out of their apartment. By this time the Denise Gardner story had hit the local newspapers. The news stories were cautiously worded and a bit short on ugly details. A discerning reader could read between the lines, however, where there were hints of mutilation, whispers of an unsolved murder, and the clear indication that a Chicago man named Robin Gecht, whose address was listed, had perpetrated it.

Yes, Wilkosz thought, there had probably been crank calls and maybe even hate letters to the Gecht family. And sadly, the Gecht kids must have been constantly taunted by other kids in the neighborhood and at school. So it was not surprising that five days after the stories hit the papers, Robin and his family moved in with Gecht's brother and sister-in-law in Carpentersville.

And it was also not surprising that Wilkosz went out to Carpentersville in turn. So certain was he that Robin Gecht was a murderous sociopath, Wilkosz talked with the Carpentersville police and shared with them the details of the Linda Sutton murder and the Denise Gardner attack. There is often a degree of territorial jealousy between police departments, but it never extended to keeping back the kind of information that might cost an unknowing officer his life.

And that's not all Wilkosz had done. A few days earlier he had ruffled a lot of territorial feathers at Area Five when he papered Chicago's West Side with flyers describing Gecht and his van and seeking information. The flyers had caused an immediate mini-panic among West Side street people. Pimps were accosting every potential trick who might resemble "the little hillbilly." Prostitutes were carrying razor knives. And every psycho in creation was calling Area Five with mysterious sightings, each of which had to be followed up, and each of which required more paperwork. Area Five, and Commanding Lieutenant John Minogue in particular, had not been pleased.

When Wilkosz found a gas station, he pulled in and called the Carpentersville chief.

"Warren?" the chief said. "You're not going to believe this. You no sooner walked out the door when Chicago showed up here with a warrant for your boy Robin Gecht!"

"A warrant? For what?"

"Let's see here," the chief said, "looks like

he cut up another hooker. Yes, here it is. Cynthia Smith. She's black. A prostitute. She went into the hospital for emergency treatment, Her breasts were all cut up. She said it was 'the hillbilly in the red van,' that he had picked her up for a date. She recognized him because she had seen him in the flyers you sent around."

Wilkosz was stunned. Could Gecht actually be going around cutting up more women even while he was out on bond and awaiting trial in the Washington case?

"I knew it," Wilkosz said. "I knew that son of a bitch was dirty for more than just Denise Gardner. So now he did another one. Damn it to hell, that is one dangerous little sociopath. But this time we'll get him. This time he's not going to walk away."

Wilkosz thanked the chief, and said he was going to drive to Chicago and go to Area Five to get more details.

"Area Five?" the chief asked. "No, this warrant says they're holding him at Area Six, not Five."

"You're sure?"

"Positive. Chicago Police Department, Area Six Detective Division."

As Wilkosz pulled back onto the highway, several thoughts roiled through his mind. This latest case had come to light because of the flyers he'd distributed, and he hoped that fact would get him back into Lieutenant Minogue's good graces.

"I'd been to Area Six before," Wilkosz says. "And as soon as I heard about this new Cynthia Smith case, the first thing I thought of was Wrigley Field, the Cubs' ballpark. Wrigley Field is in Area Six, and right around Wrigley Field is where Linda Sutton used to walk the streets, looking for customers. If it was Gecht who killed Linda Sutton, which I was sure of, then this new case meant he went right back to the same neighborhood, the same streets, to grab this newest victim. And all this while he's still awaiting trial for Gardner. The man's nerve was simply staggering. Either he thought he was invincible or he thought we were stupid. He was wrong on both counts."

Another thought, half formed, nagged at the detective until he was finally able to pull it together.

"There was a time span of about a year and a half between Linda Sutton's murder and the attack on Denise Gardner. Yet now there's only two weeks between Gardner and this new one, Smith. If he was so . . . hungry, for lack of a better word, that he'd take this kind of chance only two weeks after Denise Gardner, then it was sure as sunrise he hadn't waited a year and a half between Sutton and Gardner. He'd committed other murders. Murders we didn't know anything about. And what if we had no way to break him, no way to ever know who else he killed? That thought was driving me nuts."

As he headed toward Chicago, he was not yet sure what his next move should be. Certainly, he wouldn't be able to talk with Gecht for a while. Gecht was again in the hands of Chicago's interrogators, who had their own case against him to wrap up before they would allow the DuPage detective any further access. It was going to be a repeat of his visit two weeks ago to Area Five. This new prostitute-mutilation case would raise the stakes, and Wilkosz knew the Chicago cops would take their time in getting their new case against Gecht wrapped up neat and tight. Wilkosz, and his continuing questions about Linda Sutton, would have to wait in line.

Besides, thought Wilkosz, Robin Gecht had proved to be a slick manipulator. Gecht wasn't likely to crack just because a few cops interrogated him. Ah, but Eddie Spreitzer, Wilkosz thought, now there was a different story. He veered onto an off-ramp and headed for Chicago's West Side. Time to talk to Eddie Spreitzer.

Chapter Ten

When Warren Wilkosz pulled up in front of the Schubert Street apartment building where Eddie lived with his mother and step-father, he came upon Eddie and several other young men climbing into a car. Wil-kosz rolled down the window of his un-marked squad.

"Hey, Eddie! Spreitzer!"

Eddie looked at him. For a moment he stood still, and Wilkosz was reminded of a rabbit caught in a car's headlights. Then Eddie shifted his weight and glanced at his friends' car, as if he might run.

"Don't even think about it, Eddie," Wilkosz said. "Come on over here. I want to talk to you."

Eddie Spreitzer said a few words to his friends, who got in the car and drove off. Wil-kosz was amused to note that they came to a full, legal stop at the corner and then used their turn signal to go left.

Eddie Spreitzer walked slowly toward Wilkosz's car, stopping about ten feet from the driver's window.

"How's it going, Eddie?" Wilkosz asked.

"Okay. But I didn't do nothin' this time."

This time? Wilkosz motioned him over. "So, what are you up to, Eddie? Who's your friends?"

"Just guys. But I didn't do nothin'."

"So you said. Get in the car, Eddie."

"Why? Why do I gotta get in the car? I told you already, I didn't do nothin'."

"Just get in," Wilkosz said flatly.

Spreitzer opened the door and climbed in.

"So, Eddie," Wilkosz said, "what do you know about your boss getting picked up again?"

"What do you mean?"

"I mean he was picked up again. They say he cut up another prostitute."

Eddie Spreitzer stared open-mouthed. Then he seemed to rouse himself. "So? So what? I don't know nothin' about it. It's got nothin' to do with me, and I got nothin' to do with it. I ain't even seen Robin."

"No? What have you been doing with yourself, then?"

"Just, you know, hanging, hanging out with my friends. That's all. I ain't done nothin' bad."

"I see," Wilkosz said. "Well, I'm on my way

in to get the details of this new thing they say Robin's done. Maybe you'd like to come along."

With this, Spreitzer started squirming on his seat and shaking his head back and forth. Again, Wilkosz was struck by the image of Eddie as a puppet. Spreitzer grabbed the door handle, as though he meant to bolt from the car. "I don't want to go in! I don't want to go to the police station, and anyway, I ain't done nothin'."

Wilkosz could see that Eddie was overwrought. It was as if some invisible power were whispering in Eddie's ear: "Just keep your mouth shut."

"Okay, okay," Wilkosz said. "Just relax." He could see that Eddie's fists were balled so tightly they were turning white.

"Why me?" Eddie shouted. "Why don't you guys pick on somebody else?"

"Nobody's picking on you, Eddie. You're free to leave."

"Huh?"

"I said you're free to leave."

Eddie grabbed for the door.

"But, Eddie," Wilkosz said, "you better stick close to home because the Chicago detectives are going to want to talk to you, too. In fact, Eddie, you know what I'd do if I were you? I'd go on into the station voluntarily. This afternoon, you know, to clear yourself with the detectives on this new case before they have to come out looking for you."

"Sure," Eddie said. "Good idea. Thanks." Then he was gone.

Ten minutes later, Wilkosz was sitting in the second-floor detective squad room with Chicago detective Phil Murphy.

"Coffee?" Murphy asked.

Wilkosz nodded, smiling. There wasn't a whole lot that he or most other cops did without a cup of coffee nearby, a habit developed over many years of working around-the-clock and graveyard shifts.

"It's a Riverview case," Murphy said. He stood by a hot plate, pouring the inky, bitter brew into styrofoam cups.

"Riverview" meant Area Six, an area covering all of Chicago's north lakefront. Gecht, Murphy explained to Wilkosz as he brought over the coffee, had been taken to the sprawling glass-and-steel Area Six headquarters that had been built on the site of Chicago's beloved old amusement park. Riverview Park, named after the Chicago River, had been to the Windy City what Coney Island was to New York, and many of the cops who worked at Area Six had their own teenage memories of Saturday night dates under the carny lights.

"So. Sorry to tell you this, pal," Murphy said, "but you're third in line." He sat across from Wilkosz on the other side of a small wooden table. "Area Five has to wait until Area Six is done with Gecht before we can talk to him. Then you have to wait for us."

Both men shrugged and continued talking. The delay was inevitable, a part of the job. Whoever had the cause-of-arrest case against the perpetrator "owned" him until they were satisfied, and all police officers understand and respect that.

Still, Murphy gave Wilkosz as much help as he could. With two or three other detectives standing around in the squad room, he laid out the details of the Cynthia Smith attack.

"You know, of course, that Smith identified Gecht from one of your flyers?"

"Yes," Wilkosz said tensely. He had caught some flak about papering the streets outside his jurisdiction, and now Gecht was back in custody as a result of those flyers. He was glad that he'd had a part in wrapping the net around Robin Gecht a little tighter, but this was no time for an "I told you so."

Murphy narrowed his eyes at him and nodded. Wilkosz wasn't sure if the nod meant "good work" or "you're one lucky son of a bitch."

Information is coin of the realm in police stations, and when Murphy was done, Wilkosz paid in kind with information of his own. He told the detectives about his latest talk with Eddie Spreitzer.

"Spreitzer is breakable, no doubt about that," Murphy said. "And he's dirty. No doubt about that either. We've got a car out looking for him right now."

Then Murphy stood up. He looked at Wilkosz, as if he were taking the measure of the man. Finally, he went to his desk. In a minute he came back with a thick manila folder. "Take a look at this," he said, handing Wilkosz the folder.

"What is it?"

"Another case we want to talk to Gecht about. Since you're looking at him for a possible homicide, I figure you have a right to see it."

Wilkosz opened the folder. It contained a deviate sexual assault case report filed back on June 13 by a young black woman. She had given her name at the time as Angel York, but Wilkosz knew that didn't mean too much. Prostitutes take pride in the wide range of names they use. Often they will pick names that they think sound elegant or fancy; sometimes they simply look at the arresting officer's nameplate and use that.

Page one of the report had been handwritten by the uniformed patrol officer who made the first report of a crime. The rest of it had been typed by the follow-up investigators.

But even on the first page, certain words leaped out at Wilkosz as he scanned the neatly boxed descriptions: "Vehicle: Van— red in color, dark-tinted windows. Offender: M/W/5'7", brown hair, thin build, light oily complexion, blue eyes, black square-toed hightop shoes with side zippers." Wilkosz looked up at Murphy, who raised his eyebrows and nodded. Then Wilkosz looked back down at the report, to the box labeled VICTIM INJURIES.

"Lacerations to the left breast," he read aloud.

"Sound a bit familiar?" Murphy asked with a grim smile. "We've been going through all our sex-offense cases looking for possibles on our guy, and we came across this from back in June. Go ahead, read it, and tell me Robin Gecht isn't one sick-ass, scary little bastard."

Wilkosz scanned quickly through the pages and then started over. By his second reading, he had a clear picture of what had happened to nineteen-year-old Angel York on the night of June 13. And it was hideous.

Chapter Eleven

Angel was only nineteen, but she was experienced in the ways of the street. So when she saw squad cars cruising slowly down North Avenue, and then a few minutes later saw them cruising back up the other way, she knew what was going down—a sweep.

This strip along North Avenue was known for its heavy hooker traffic. Angel had no intention of spending the night in jail. It was only 3:00 A.M. The taverns would close at four, bringing her a rush of business, and then after that would come the early dawn construction crews, and then the big business of the day, the suburban commuters. What constituted "rush hour" for traffic constituted rush hour for the street prostitutes, too.

Angel ducked into an alley as the squads cruised past again. Just then a red van pulled slowly past the mouth of the alley. It was the driver's third or fourth pass, and

Angel knew he was looking for a date. She peered out, looking down the street. The squads were making U-turns and heading back. Angel ran to the van.

Pulling open the passenger door, she jumped in and opened her mouth to offer her standard sex-for-money routine, but instead she found herself staring into the barrel of a blue steel .45.

The skinny, greasy-haired white guy stared at her, and his blue eyes were cold. "Sit still," he said, "and shut up." She did. He drove for several blocks before pulling to the curb in the 1400 block of North Cleaver, a neighborhood of factories and light industry, deserted at this hour.

Still holding the gun to Angel's head, he ordered her through a plywood door into the rear of the van, then told her to take her clothes off. Quickly, he tied her feet together. Then he reached up onto a shelf and pulled out handcuffs. "Kneel!"

He cuffed her right hand to her left foot and her left hand to a shelf support. Then he tore off a strip of duct tape and pasted it across her mouth.

He pulled a pair of panty hose off a shelf, and, kneeling in front of her, he wound the panty hose over and over around her breasts, forcing them to protrude. He did all this quickly and efficiently, and with no conversation or obvious show of emotion.

He sat back, looking her over. Nodding, he stood and stripped off his clothes. Then he took a huge knife down from a shelf and again knelt in front of her.

He uncuffed her left hand and stared at her. Then he reached out with his right index finger and traced a line, again and again, along the outer curve of her left breast. Holding the .45 to her head, he put the knife into her left hand. Then he traced the line again with his finger.

"Cut it."

Angel couldn't believe she'd heard right. "I can't," she tried to say against the tape tight across her mouth.

"I said cut it," he said again, and jammed the gun against her temple, knocking her over sideways.

Now Angel began to hyperventilate from shock, and she could hardly breathe against the tape. Her hands trembled as she lifted the knife. She touched it to the outer rim of her breast.

"Cut it," he demanded, wild eyed now and intently focused.

Angel held her breath and nicked a small incision, hoping the sight of blood would be enough for him. Pain shot through her whole body. She felt faint.

"More!" he screamed, jamming the gun against the side of her head.

She was reeling now, but she drove the knife in again, falling nearly unconscious as she did it.

He reared back in frustration, then reached forward and ripped the wound wide open. Angel's screams were muffled against the tape.

He tormented her this way for an hour. When it was finally over, he slapped a piece of duct tape over the gaping wound in Angel's breast, and warned her that he knew who she was and if she went to the police, he would come for her and kill her. Then he opened the back door of the van and threw her out, headfirst, into an alley. As the van sped off, Angel staggered to her feet and started running. Later, she was found on Grand Avenue by a passing security guard. She was hysterical and bleeding profusely through the duct tape on her left breast. The guard put her in his car and dropped her off at St. Elizabeth's Hospital.

Doctors were able to save Angel's breast, and they turned over to detectives their findings that evidence of human semen was present in the wound.

Wilkosz put the report down on the desk. He was appalled. He sipped his coffee and stood a moment to stretch and take in deep lungfuls of air. He felt as if he'd just walked through the details of Linda Sutton's death. Wilkosz turned to Detective Phil Murphy.

"I take it you've picked this York up?"

Murphy shook his head. "I wish to God we could. We've put feelers out all over the West Side; we've notified the women's lockups and the street girls who regularly give us information. Nothing. She hasn't been seen on the street since she got out of the hospital. Our feeling is she believed he really would come after her, and she just took off. Boogied out of town. Who knows where."

Wilkosz tapped his fingers on the desk. "Gecht did this. And Gecht killed Linda Sutton."

Murphy shrugged as he picked up their styrofoam cups and walked toward the coffee machine.

"No doubt you're right," he said. "Now all we have to do is prove it."

Chapter Twelve

It was Saturday morning. Eddie Spreitzer had spent the night in jail. Now he sat in Interrogation Room F at Area Five, facing Assistant State's Attorney Richard Beuke and Detective Tom Flynn. He was ready to talk, and on the record. He felt that he had been involved in some terrible things, he said, and he wanted to tell somebody about them.

"Just answer in your own words," Beuke told him after explaining Eddie's rights and the questioning procedure. "Just tell us, as truthfully as you can, what happened."

The questioning of Eddie Spreitzer by Flynn and Beuke went on for the next several hours. It was a tedious process. Spreitzer was slow, he was afraid, and he was easily led. The detectives had to be careful that none of Eddie's confession was a result of anything they suggested to him. Making the process even more difficult, every few minutes Eddie tended to wander off into irrelevancies. At times the detectives felt he was doing it deliberately to avoid zero-ing in on any specific questions, and they would try to nudge him back on course.

But at other times they would sit back and listen to Eddie babble about how he and Robin were· in business together and how they were going to expand and become something really important. This was a re-current theme, the illusion that he was about to become a *somebody.* Psychiatrists call that sort of delusion "magical thinking," the belief that if one tries hard enough to believe something, even something impossi-ble, he can make it come true.

Whenever Eddie would wander too close to the truth of his mundane life, he veered off into the "somebody important" wonderland, like a child who reaches for its security blan-ket when the lights go off. And dominating this self-delusion was the figure of Eddie's fearsome hero/master, Robin Gecht.

At 8:30 A.M., a court reporter was sum-moned to join Flynn, Beuke, and Eddie for a formal confession. It is fairly standard practice to have one cop with the A.S.A. at a confession. More cops might spook the suspect with too many power figures, but at least one is necessary so that two people are always witnesses to a confession.

For the record, Beuke again read Eddie his constitutional rights, known as the Miranda

Warning, and each of the participants signed each page as the court reporter printed it out.

Beuke then began to put formal questions to Eddie:

BEUKE: I want to direct your attention to October 6th of 1982, at about 1:30 in the morning hours. Can you tell us where you were at that time?

SPREITZER: We were on North Avenue going toward Damen.

Q: We? Who were you with, Ed?

A: Robin Gecht.

Q: How long have you known Robin?

A: Almost two years.

Q: At that time were you living with Robin?

A: Yes.

Q: Okay. When you were going down Damen and North Avenue, were you in a van?

A: Yes.

Q: Can you describe that van for me, Ed?

A: It was a '74, '75 Dodge van, red on the outside, with silver bumpers, and on the inside it had red and black carpeting on the top, and brown paneling on the doors. And it had a roach clip with light blue feathers hanging from the carpet that was over the window.

Q: At that time, Eddie, were you driving the van or was Robin driving the van?

A: I was.

Q: Whose van was that?

A: It was Robin's.

Q: Now, when you got to the area around North Avenue and Damen, did you have occasion to see any men?

A: We seen three people.

Q: Where were they standing?

A: They were standing on the—on the corner by the telephone booth down Damen Avenue.

Q: When you saw these men standing a couple blocks away, did Robin say anything to you?

A: Yes. He told me to turn right and go real slow, 'cause he went into the back to get the .38 pistol and the rifle that were in back.

Q: Did you see Robin get a pistol?

A: Yes.

Q: What kind of pistol was it?

A: It was a .38. He went to the little sliding cabinet drawer in the van. He got shells for the pistol.

Q: Did he load the gun?

A: Yes, he did.

Q: You also mentioned a rifle. Did you see where he got the rifle?

A: He got that from back next to the cabinet, underneath the light blue blanket that it was wrapped up in.

Q: Now, as Robin was loading the pistol and getting the rifle, were you driving the van?

A: Yes, I was going real slow.

Q: Were you proceeding toward the three men?

A: Yes. He told me to go up toward them a

little faster and when I got up to them, he told me to stop. He rolled down the window, he had the pistol in his hand.

Q: Okay, what did Robin do when you stopped the van?

A: He rolled down the window real fast, pointed the gun to the three guys that was standing by the telephone, and opened fire on them.

Q: Did you—how many shots did Robin fire?

A: He fired five shots.

Q: Did you see any of the three men get hit?

A: I seen one guy hit the sidewalk and one guy fell toward the telephone. The other one ran away.

As the interview with Eddie continued, Flynn and Beuke exchanged frequent glances, but showed no other reaction. Both were familiar with the Damen/North Avenue shooting, but no one had put it down to a random killing. The area was heavily Puerto Rican, and several gangs were at constant war over the lucrative drug trade. Drive-by shootings were a fairly recent phenomenon, but were not unknown to the area.

The man who "fell toward the phone booth" had been Rafael Tirado. He had been shot in the back, in the left cheek, and in the throat. He died where he fell. The man who "hit the sidewalk" had been Albert Rosario. He had been shot in the head just above the left eye. Despite extensive brain surgery, Rosario had been paralyzed and doctors had told him he would spend the rest of his life in a wheelchair.

The interview continued. Now it seemed Eddie couldn't stop talking. He told them Robin had picked up a black hooker after shooting the men at the phone booth.

"Robin ordered me into the back of the van. I couldn't see anything, but I heard them discussing price for a blow job. Robin gave the girl some pills."

Eddie went on to say that he heard sounds of sex from the front of the van, and then "two little taps on the floor."

Q: Did those two little taps on the floor mean anything to you?
A: Yeah, it was a signal for me to go out through the back door and go to the side door.
Q: Had you and Robin planned that before you picked up this hooker?
A: Yes, we did.
Q: Had you used that signal with Robin on any other occasion?
A: Yes, we did.
Q: How many times?
A: Lots of times.
Q: When you picked up women?
A: Yes.

Eddie described how he had waited outside the van while Robin was in the back with the hooker. Then Robin opened the rear doors and pulled the young woman out into the alley. She couldn't stand up, and Eddie could see she was high from the pills. Both men pulled all her clothes off, except for her panties and shoes.

"Now, Eddie," Beuke said, "I want you to tell me in detail about the place where this happened."

How far into the alley were they? Beuke asked. How many feet from the railroad tracks? How far from the factory? The details were important because only someone who'd actually been there would know such specifics. Eddie was, in police parlance, "placing himself at the scene," an important consideration if he later claimed to have been coerced into his confession.

q: Did Robin have anything in his hand?
a: Yeah, he had a knife in his hand.
q: Do you remember how long the blade on that knife was, Eddie?
a: It was about seven or eight inches, with a brown handle.
q: Okay. Did Robin do anything with that knife?
a: He cut, you know, one of her breasts off.

Eddie said Robin had sex with the wound

in the woman's chest, and then with the severed breast. He said Robin then ordered him to go back to the van and bring another knife, a four-incher with a jagged blade. Eddie said he gave that knife to Robin and then went back to wait by the van.

Q: Did Robin come back to the van a short time later?
A: About five, ten minutes later. He had the knives—he was holding the knife, and I think he had one of the—I think he had the breast with him.
Q: You think he did?
A: He did.
Q: And what did he do with the breast?
A: He kept it in the van. He put it on the floor between the seats.

By this time it was clear from the date and detailed description that the woman Eddie Spreitzer was describing was Denise Gardner. It was an amazing revelation; Eddie Spreitzer had been there when Gecht mutilated Denise Gardner, and the victim herself hadn't even known it. She had been so drugged that the last thing she remembered was passing out inside the van.

Earlier, Eddie had told Beuke that "something else happened" in late August, which would have been two months before the

Gardner attack. Now Beuke asked him, "Eddie, what happened in late August?"

Eddie said that he and Robin had been driving around in the red van at about 2:00 A.M. looking for another black hooker. At North Avenue and the Chicago River, they found one. Robin pulled over and Eddie got into the rear of the van. The girl climbed in and Robin started talking to her about all the pills he had. He said they wouldn't hurt her, they would just make her "horny." Robin and the girl then discussed various sexual acts and prices, and when they reached agreement, Robin started up the van and drove off.

They drove for a few minutes and then Eddie heard two taps on the floor. He got out of the rear of the van, taking a knife with him.

Q: Now, what happened when Robin got around by the passenger door?
A: He pulled her out of the van, tossed her up alongside the van.
Q: Did Robin have anything in his hands?
A: Yeah. Handcuffs.
Q: Was she handcuffed with her hands in front of her or in back of her?
A: In back of her.

Eddie said that he and Robin ripped the girl's clothes off and dragged her under the bridge, where passing traffic couldn't see them. He said Robin forced the girl to sit on

top of him for intercourse, while she per-
formed fellatio on Eddie, who was standing
above them. Then Robin asked him if they
were having fun yet. Eddie said no and Robin
asked him what he was going to do about it.

At that point, according to Eddie, he
pulled out a four-inch pocketknife and
stabbed the girl several times in the chest.
Then, he said, he felt nauseated and he
threw the knife into the river and went back
to the van. He said he didn't know what happened between Robin and the girl after that,
but that a few minutes later, Robin got back
into the van and they drove home.

When Eddie finished his description of his
crime, there was silence in the room. The
young court reporter had become pale.

At this point Detective Flynn slipped out
of the room and told the other detectives
what was going on. He described the attack
Eddie Spreitzer had just confessed to.

"Check the files," he said. "A hooker murder at North and the River. Body was probably recovered under the bridge."

Flynn was back in the closed interrogation
room when a file was found and brought to
him. It was a file on the murder of a young
woman named Sandra Delaware. She was
nineteen years old.

Chapter Thirteen

When Detective Flynn read the Delaware file, he learned that on the morning of August 17, 1982, three young Hispanic men had been walking along the bank of the Chicago River, looking for aluminum cans. What they found, under the North Avenue bridge, was a body. Police arrived on the scene at 10:50.

The body was lying on the east bank of the river. The victim, naked, was lying on her back. Her wrists were bound together with a blue shoelace, her ankles with the matching lace. No shoes were found. A bra was tied around her neck with a knot in the throat area. She was wearing a yellow metal neck chain with a blue and white charm.

Police officers, not being jewelers, are always careful not to report that any piece of jewelry is "silver" or "gold." It is simply white metal or yellow metal. The same applies to gems. A diamond is a "white stone," a ruby is a "red stone." This helps to avoid lawsuits that would result if a piece of jewelry described by a police officer as "diamonds and gold" turned out to be base metal and cut glass.

The investigators at Sandra Delaware's death scene found blood smears on her upper left thigh, right arm and shoulder, and right breast. A huge pool of still-liquid blood had spread into the grass from under her buttocks and seeped down through the weeds and into the brown water. They estimated that she had been dead for about six hours.

As word of the murder under the bridge spread, a foreman at a nearby factory reported finding a purse in the parking lot. The only things in the purse were several papers, including bond slips, in the name of Sandy Harris, and "numerous red tinfoil packets containing prophylactics." A quick check through the Identification Section downtown verified that Sandra Delaware also used the name Sandy Harris.

Virtually all street hookers use false names, some of them having been arrested thirty or forty times under thirty or forty different names. They don't do it to hide their real identities from the police, since they know quite well that their real identity will be established through fingerprints. Perhaps the name game lets them pretend to be someone else, someone whose life really is glamorous, even if only for the few minutes it takes them to speak the name and for the officer to write it down. Jane Smith doesn't exist for those few moments, but Sparkle Diamond does.

The detectives who initially investigated Sandra Delaware's death had little to go on, which was usually the case when prostitutes were found murdered. A working girl's contacts were so fleeting, so anonymous, that it was impossible to know who might have developed a grudge against her.

When the detectives began asking questions on the street, however, they came up with a name, *Freddie "Minister" Johnson, a known pimp. Sandra had worked for him until they had an argument the year before and Sandra had left and found herself a new man. The Minister had been coming around lately, threatening to kill Sandra, her new man, and even her elderly grandmother unless she came back to work for him.

Detectives talked to Sandra's sister, who said she and Sandra had not been close for several years because of Sandra's lifestyle, but still, she and her family had been afraid to walk the streets after the Minister issued his threats. According to the sister, the Minister was a high-ranking member of the

Black Gangster Disciples, a vicious and so-phisticated Chicago street gang.

Sandra had been a lucrative property, and because of her, and several others like her, the Minister was able to drive around in his metal-flake bronze Olds Toronado or his Pepto-Bismol pink Cadillac, make his drug deals, lounge around with his friends, and generally live the good life. In all the many times Sandra Delaware had been arrested for working the streets, never once had the Minis-ter posted the $50 bond for her early release, leaving her instead to spend the night huddled under the bullpen's steel bench.

The Minister was brought in for ques-tioning, and he made an event of the occa-sion, bowing and strutting his way through the station like a visiting pasha. The Minis-ter claimed that the night Delaware was murdered, he'd been at a far Northside motel with another of his ladies, one of Sandra Delaware's "wife-in-laws," as the women who belong to one man call each other. The wife-in-law was brought in, and she verified the Minister's alibi, as did the motel man-ager. The Minister was released.

Police had pursued several other leads, but nothing new developed in the case.

Until now. Detective Flynn put down the file, wondering what other unsolved murders Eddie Spreitzer knew about.

Chapter Fourteen

Ironically, while Eddie was implicating Robin
Gecht in crimes that the Area Five detectives
didn't even know about, the Area Six case
against Robin Gecht was falling apart. The
accusing prostitute, Cynthia Smith, had
seen Wilkosz's flyer, as had all the street
people, and she kept insisting it was the
"hillbilly" who'd attacked and cut her. But
Smith couldn't come up with one bit of information beyond what was contained in the
flyer.

Area Six detectives became suspicious and
pressed her for details. She became evasive.
She said she was sick. She demanded to be
taken to the hospital, a frequent demand of
working girls, who know that state jail standards require a trip to the hospital for whoever requests it, even if there is patently
nothing wrong with them. For many of them,
these trips represent the only medical care
they ever receive.

But hookers also pull this routine when they want to avoid questioning. They know that once at the hospital, they can invent symptoms interesting enough to require many hours of time-consuming tests. The Area Six detectives knew that was exactly the situation here. Cynthia Smith was lying about how she had sustained her injuries. Maybe her man had cut her and she didn't want to turn him in. Maybe she had cut herself for some reason. Maybe she wanted to get on television or get pampered treatment as an important witness against "the hillbilly." Maybe all sorts of things, but there was no maybe about the fact that the Area Six case against Robin Gecht was evaporating.

However, at this particular time Robin Gecht was not the foremost case for Area Six detectives. They were working in the glare of an international spotlight, under intense pressure to solve a murder case that had shocked the entire country.

One week earlier, a beautiful young stewardess named Paula Prince, who kept an apartment in the fashionable Near North Loop, Wells and LaSalle Street area, had taken two Tylenol capsules, and fallen dead to the bathroom floor. Cyanide poisoning. With her death the Chicago Police Department, and Area Six in particular, inherited the most notorious anonymous murder case in Chicago's history. By the time prostitute Cynthia Smith was undergoing hospital tests for undefinable complaints, six more people had been killed by cyanide-contaminated Tylenol capsules.

The news media, ignoring Gecht for the moment, went berserk over the Tylenol murders. Product-tampering was a brand-new horror on the landscape, and the ramifications were staggering. Billions of over-the-counter medications, none of them yet tamper-proof, were stocked on grocery and drugstore shelves across the country. Now that some maniac had invented this insidious new crime, might not others take up the challenge? And if bottles of pills could be poisoned right on the store shelves, why not bottles of apple juice, or baby food, or . . . anything?

News crews from Japan, Germany, France, England, Australia, from virtually every country in the world, poured into Chicago. Every major American news outlet, print, audio, and video, headed into the city. They flooded the downtown hotels, colliding with one another for room space. And they all converged, every day, on Area Six. Huge black limousines bearing star reporters, their vans and technical crews following, fought through traffic for exclusive front-row space. The less stellar and less wealthy members of the fourth estate piled and squeezed into taxis downtown for the daily hike to Area Six. Local reporters drove themselves to the police station every morning, often with plans to spend the day. Not overly concerned about the ordinary people who had business to conduct at the station, reporters' cars were pulled up on sidewalks, blocked driveways and fire lanes, parking lot exits and entrances.

Johnson & Johnson, the parent company of Tylenol, responded immediately to the crisis, ordering all of its various Tylenol products recalled from the shelves. City Hall at first told people to bring their home supplies of Tylenol to the nearest police station. But the turn-ins quickly grew from hundreds of bottles to thousands. Since no one knew if the product had been poisoned at the manufacturer's source, not just Tylenol capsules but all Tylenol products were being collected and turned in. The Chicago Health Department soon had warehouses full of Tylenol products.

Illinois Attorney General Tyrone Fahner quickly stepped to the forefront of the Tylenol investigation and began holding daily press conferences at Area Six, wherein he hinted at tips and clues that were being developed. He kept promising the world a quick arrest, to the dismay of Chicago police officials, who knew they had nothing at all. As the days went by and the press conferences continued and nothing happened, the Chicago media, always quick to attack, began snidely referring to the attorney general as "Tylenol Ty" and finally "Ty-Ty." In the firestorm of media smirking and criticism, he would lose the next election and retire to private practice. The Tylenol poisoning case has never been solved.

It was in this circus atmosphere that Area Six detectives, who had taken to parking their personal cars blocks away and walking to the station, continued their investigation into the activities of Robin Gecht. They were in constant phone contact with Area Five, of course, where Eddie Spreitzer was leading detectives through the details of one horrific murder after another. Every nightmare scenario that Eddie laid out featured his boss, Robin Gecht, as the instigator of the hunt as well as the primary killer. The detectives at Area Six promised to wrap up their case against Gecht, one way or another, as soon as possible, so they could turn Gecht over to Area Five.

Meanwhile, in the second-floor squad room at Area Five, small groups of detectives kept each other abreast of the latest revelations coming out of Interrogation Room F.

Each time a new detective team would enter the room, briefcases in hand, to sit down at a typewriter, someone already there would bring the new men up to date on whatever case Eddie was talking about now. Since Chicago averages about eight hundred murders a year, all the detective teams had unsolved case files of their own.

Warren Wilkosz was caught up in the room's growing tension, just like all the Chicago detectives milling around, but he also knew he was in a different position than the rest. Each new Chicago case in which Eddie Spreitzer was implicating himself and Robin Gecht would entail yet another full-blown paper trail for the Area Five detectives, another case to be built before they could allow Wilkosz to step in with his questions about the Linda Sutton murder. He knew he had no more important task than to be right here, waiting his turn, but that didn't make the wait easier.

Wilkosz knew, as all the detectives did, that the window of opportunity could close at any time. Eddie Spreitzer could suddenly decide to stop talking, or he could change his mind and demand an attorney. Any defense attorney would say, as the first words out of his mouth: "Eddie, shut up. Not one more word to the police about anything." And that would be that.

Thus, Wilkosz was staring out the rain-streaked window, his thoughts in synch with the somber weather, when he heard his name. Surprised, he turned and saw Tom Flynn motioning him toward the other end of the long squad room, just outside Interrogation Room F.

"Don't tell me he's confessing to Sutton," Wilkosz said as he walked toward Flynn. "I can't believe my guardian angel would be that kind to me."

"Your guardian angel may just be in love with you today, Warren." Flynn smiled. The tall, silver-haired detective was weary after the long hours of intense cat-and-mouse questioning at the degree of human depravity he'd been forced to absorb.

"Eddie may have given himself and Gecht up on your Sutton case," Flynn said. "But he's talking about having killed so many different black hookers, he's having trouble separating the details of one from another. And so are we."

"What, then?" Wilkosz asked, wondering why he'd been called over.

"Did you guys have a girl disappear out of a shopping center last spring? May, probably. On a Saturday morning, out in Elmhurst?"

"Good Lord! Lorry Borowski!"

"What's her name again?" Flynn asked, taking out his notepad.

"Lorraine Ann Borowski. Pretty little thing. Twenty-one years old, she was snatched up on her way to work. We just recovererd her bones two months ago out in an abandoned cemetery. Are you telling me these guys killed Lorry Borowski?"

"Sure looks like it. Eddie's telling us he and Robin cruised the streets all night, looking for any woman walking alone so they could snatch her off the street. They didn't score, and they pulled into a shopping center parking lot that morning. That's when they saw her walking through the parking lot by herself."

Flynn turned to head back into Interrogation Room F. "You probably want to get on the horn to your office. We're going to need corroborating details and . . ."

But Warren Wilkosz was already walking toward the telephone. As he dialed, a profound sadness washed over him. He remembered that Lorry Ann's father had continued to pay her rent for a long time after she disappeared, hoping against hope that his "baby girl" would come home again. Wilkosz also remembered Mrs. Borowski telling him about a little, pencil-scrawled poem by Christina Rossetti that Lorry Ann always carried in her wallet. The poem read:

Hurt no living thing, ladybird, nor butterfly,
Nor moth with dusty wing, nor cricket chirping
cheerily,
Nor grasshopper so light of leap, nor dancing gnat,
Nor beetle fat,
Nor harmless worms that creep.

Chapter Fifteen

May 15, 1982

The bedroom community of suburban Elmhurst, a lovely tree-lined town sixteen miles west of Chicago, stirred to life in the early sunshine. Clock radios buzzed, and soon the aromas of coffee and bacon wafted from open kitchen windows. Shortly after eight o'clock on this Saturday morning, Lorraine Ann Borowski left the St. Charles West apartment complex for the short walk to her secretary's job at ReMax East-West, Inc., a realty office on St. Charles Road.

Lorry Ann, as her family called her, was a radiantly pretty girl. Slim, tan, perky, and just five feet three, she had a sparkle and a smile that turned men's heads. Having been raised in a loving and lovely home, Lorry Ann had grown up to become a generous and considerate young woman. She and her five sisters and brothers had brought home all kinds of strays over the years, and their big-hearted parents had let the kids keep most of them. The family had raised over the years six parakeets, a mud turtle, a white shepherd dog, endless stray cats, several fantail pigeons, and a whole flock of ducks.

Lorry Ann had been working for ReMax part-time in the afternoons for a month, but now one of the other secretaries was leaving and Lorry Ann was starting full-time work. She was happy about it, even about working Saturdays.

Part of Lorry Ann's job was to make sure the office was open by eight-thirty, since an owner-manager would show up by eight forty-five to pick up keys to homes for sale. As Lorry Ann walked across the small shopping plaza, she had reason to be optimistic about her life, and she took no notice of the red Dodge van that started up and began a slow circle of the parking lot.

Young Lorry Ann looked trim and lovely in her green slacks and white ruffled blouse. She waved hello to other people opening up their shops. A young man at the cleaners had been wanting to ask her for a date, but he still didn't have the nerve. He waved to her and she waved back and smiled, as she always did.

A few minutes later, the ReMax owner-manager, Donald Stibbe, arrived at his office and was surprised to find that the door was still locked and the lights were off. Lorry was such a dependable girl. As he fished in his pocket for his key, he noticed some small items on the ground at the edge of the parking area. Someone must have dropped them while getting out of a car, he thought, but he paid them no further attention.

Once he opened for business, Stibbe called Lorry's apartment, but no one answered. He made a few more calls to set up appointments for the day, but he kept wondering about his secretary. When one of his agents arrived, she mentioned the items on the sidewalk. She and Stibbe decided to pick them up in case the owner came back for them.

There were two small cosmetic cases, eyeshadow and blusher; some coins; a keyring; and, oddly, a pair of women's tan leather shoes. Not far away was a red-handled flathead screwdriver. Stribbe and the real estate agent brought them inside and laid them on a desk. It was then they saw that the key ring had the company's name. Could it belong to Lorry? Hoping he was wrong, Stibbe tried several keys on the front lock. One of them fit.

Stibbe called Elmhurst police, and from the start they decided to treat this as a possible abduction. It was easy to imagine a young woman suddenly dropping her keys and rushing off for some reason. But the fact that her shoes had been left behind was very troubling.

Major crimes were not common in Elmhurst. The suburb averaged only two murders a year, and even those were usually the result of a bar fight, so police threw everything they could into this investigation. The officers learned that Lorry Ann shared an apartment with a young man, *Mike Battaglia. Though she and Mike divided the expenses, they were friends, not lovers. Lorry had boyfriends, but Mike was not one of them.

Mike told police he worked nights for the Chicago & Northwestern Railway. He had come home at nine-thirty that morning and Lorry was gone, presumably for work. He said that, judging from her room, she hadn't slept there the night before. The officers, though, found cosmetics scattered around the bathroom wash basin, a hand-held hair dryer on her bed, and a damp towel on the floor. Lorry had been there, all right, and she had showered, done her hair, put on her makeup, and left the apartment that morning apparently as if this were just another day.

Lorry Ann's family was frantic. Her parents also lived in Elmhurst, and her mother told police that Lorry Ann had come over the day before on her ten-speed bike and was upset. She told her mother that a "big, giant man" had been following her in a car and that she stopped at a gas station, pretending to need air in her tires, just so she could ask the attendant for help. Lorry Ann told her mother that the attendant had come out of the gas station and gone toward the parking islands, intending to tell the man to leave. Then, the heavy-set man had driven off.

Detective Commander John Millner, who had taken immediate charge of the case, ordered a canvass of every gas station between the apartment complex and Mrs. Borowski's home, but police found no attendant who remembered the incident.

Other officers interviewed dozens of employees at the shops in the plaza. The manager of the Nautilus Fitness Center recalled seeing keys and cosmetics on the pavement when he came to work. There was "an older model" silver car and "an orange van" in the lot, he said. The owner of a pet store remembered the "orange van," because he had a similar model, a 1976 Dodge Tradesman.

Other employees in the plaza shops spoke of a suspicious young man on a motorcycle, odd telephone calls, customers asking strange questions, and drivers who just didn't seem right. Every possible lead had to be checked out, and every one became a dead end.

Detectives began probing Lorry Ann's personal life. She was pretty and she was popular. She dated several young men, and her girlfriends reported their theories about hurt feelings here, wounded egos there, previous quarrels, public scenes and private confessions. Boyfriends past and present were interviewed. No one could come up with a motive, except that Lorry Ann was attractive.

On Sunday, the day after Lorry vanished, Elmhurst Detective Jim O'Brien prepared a bulletin describing Lorry and the circumstances of her disappearance. On Monday, Millner issued the bulletin to groceries, drugstores, and other small businesses in Elmhurst. The information made the front page of the suburban papers, and the story about the missing young woman was carried in both the *Chicago Tribune* and the *Chicago Sun-Times*. It was unusual for the Chicago papers to carry a detailed story about a missing suburbanite; that they did was an indication of the fear everybody had about the outcome of this disappearance.

Calls flooded the Elmhurst police switchboard, many from people who claimed they had seen Lorry after the time she disappeared. On May 19, a humid Wednesday, an off-duty officer called the station and told the desk sergeant that a liquor store owner had information that sounded really good. Detectives went to Keane Liquors, just down the parking lot from ReMax.

The owner said he had arrived for work at eight-thirty Saturday and seen some kind of struggle at the side of a car to the north of the lot. The passenger door of the gray or dull silver car had been open, and a young woman had been struggling with someone inside. The liquor store owner could only see the woman over the hood, but he described her as in her mid to late twenties and with blondish-brown hair. She had possibly been wearing a yellow sleeveless blouse. The store owner couldn't see who was in the car at all, and had no idea if the person was a man or a woman, white or black. The store owner had assumed that the struggle was some sort of domestic quarrel, and he had gone about his business.

The next day Detective Commander Millner, who was a certified hypnotist, hypnotized the liquor store owner to see if the man could remember any details. Yes, he could, but only that the car was an older model, perhaps a Thunderbird or a Cougar.

It was also on May 19 that Elmhurst police followed up what they felt was their strongest tip yet. A young man reported that sometime between nine and ten Saturday he and his friends had come out of another Elmhurst liquor store, on York Road and Fullerton, on their way to the beach. They had stopped for some beer.

As they walked toward their car, they heard "screaming and banging sounds" from the trunk of an old four-door Chevrolet Impala. Stepping closer, they saw dents forming on the trunk lid as though someone were kicking it from inside. The young man called out, asking if someone needed help. With this, the sounds and movement stopped.

Just then four Hispanic men came out of the liquor store and walked toward the Chevy, giving them a "dirty look." The Hispanics climbed into the Chevy and drove off, and the young men went on their way to the beach. But they had jotted down the license plate number just in case. They thought no more about the incident until they saw the flyers and newspaper stories about Lorry Borowski's disappearance.

Elmhurst detectives immediately ran a trace on the license number, which checked out to a Hispanic name in the Uptown community of Chicago's North Side. With Chicago police assistance, they went to the home and talked to the owner of the Chevy. The man just laughed. He had been transporting several live goats in his trunk, he explained. Live goats? The man said that he had driven out to a suburban farm outside Elmhurst to buy them, and he was bringing them home for a barbecue. The officers were surprised to hear that anybody would want to eat barbecued goat. They asked to examine the trunk of the Chevy.

The uptown man lifted his trunk lid, and the officers removed a number of long, stiff white hairs. They certainly didn't look as if they came from a twenty-one-year-old woman. Laboratory tests confirmed that they were, in fact, the body hairs of *capra chordata artiodactyla*. A goat.

The interviews continued. First, of everyone who knew Lorry Ann. Then, of everyone who moved in the same circles as she. Elmhurst authorities were fairly certain by this time that Lorry was dead. They kept thinking about the shoes. In broad daylight, in a shopping center with a half dozen people only a few yards away, a young woman had been lifted right out of her shoes, and disappeared.

Lorry Ann's family began contacting psychics in their desperate attempt to find out what had happened to her. Elmhurst detectives needed to follow up each vision or vibration, no matter what they personally thought of extrasensory perception. Acting on one psychic's mental picture, they searched every inch of a local KMart, but found nothing. They also sought out a "construction site near an anchor and a body of water." They found such a place in neighboring Westmont, but there was no trace of Lorry Ann. The detectives listened to people who claimed they'd had dreams and visions regarding Lorry Ann, for the disappearance had aroused concern across the quiet western suburbs, but these visions were nothing more than what they were reported to be, dreams.

Lorry Ann's father made up his own flyers, painstakingly piecing together decal-lettering and adding to the description his own favorite photo of his beloved "baby girl." He had a thousand flyers printed up and began distributing them himself, particularly to truckers, who promised to post them in truck stops throughout the Midwest. The Borowski home, a charming and tastefully decorated Tudor, had become an open house as steady streams of concerned friends and neighbors wandered in and out, comparing notes and updating each other on the latest developments. Mrs. Borowski remembers one incident that stuck out in her mind during those dreadful days:

"A young man came dashing in the front door," she says, "shouting that he needed some of the flyers. We handed him a stack and he thanked us and rushed back out the door. There were quite a few people in the house at the time, neighbors and so forth, and we all started asking each other who he was. Nobody knew him, nobody had seen him before, and none of us ever saw him again."

On Sunday, May 30, police talked to a Villa Park woman who called to say she had information. She had been putting gas in her car just the day before at a nearby service station when a young woman approached her at the self-service pump. The woman was plump, about five six or seven and had messy blondish-brown hair. Her eyes were red and mascara streaked. She had obviously been crying.

"Ma'am," the young woman asked her, "could you please give me a ride west on Roosevelt Road?"

The distraught stranger was carrying a loaf of bread in one hand and a single pink peony in the other. But the witness explained to her that she was going in the other direction, and she watched as the young woman wandered, crying, toward the highway, still holding her loaf of bread and her pink flower.

The Villa Park woman said that after she filled her tank and paid for the gas, she looked around, thinking about giving the stranger a ride after all, but by then the crying girl was gone.

The unknown hitchhiker could not have been Lorry Ann, the officers knew; she was too tall and heavy. But who was she? They never found out.

Police were also following up a lead that had developed the day before. A Villa Park resident complained of a strange young man who lived next to him.

The nineteen-year-old, Joseph, had an explosive temper, was heavily involved in the martial arts, and often had vicious arguments with his parents. Joseph also seemed overly fond of knives and Oriental throwing stars. He had driven an "older, silver-colored" car, at least until several weeks ago. In addition, Joseph had had several run-ins with police and had been in and out of mental hospitals lately.

The officers learned from neighbors that everything the tipster said was true. Most neighbors avoided Joseph out of fear of his aggressive, erratic behavior. And no one had seen him for two weeks, about the time Lorry Ann had disappeared. From Joseph's criminal history record, police learned that his younger brother was in prison for an abduction and homicide.

Joseph's sister was open and cooperative with police and said that Joseph was a "slow starter when it comes to girls." He had been released from the Alexian Brothers psychiatric hospital on Friday, May 14, the day before Lorry Ann Borowski disappeared. But, the sister said, he probably was driving a friend's copper-colored car and not a silver one. He didn't have a car of his own. Even so, the young man seemed a good suspect.

Police found Joseph at his parents' home. On May 30, he was brought in for questioning. He appeared willing to cooperate, but detectives saw that he clearly was a very disturbed young man. He looked at Lorry Ann's photo and said he knew her. First he said he had only seen her around the neighborhood. A short while later, he said he had dated Lorry for a time but never kissed her. Then he told the officers that Lorry only liked guys with nice cars, and he didn't have one. He had to drive a friend's. He seemed irrationally bitter about this.

As the interview continued, Joseph became more and more confused about what he knew and didn't know. The detectives couldn't even get a clear idea whom he considered his best friend. Every time they asked him this question, he would name someone and would then launch into all the grievances he had against that "friend." The troubled factory worker was not ruled out as a suspect, but police didn't get the feeling that they were talking to a possible killer. On his report one of the detectives noted dryly: "Subject was not logical with this investigator."

Further interviews showed that Joseph's alibi for Saturday, May 15, checked out, and on June 4 he passed a lie-detector test administered by Detective Commander Millner. Lorry Ann had been missing for three weeks, and the detectives were back to square one.

Chapter Sixteen

November 6, 1982

Warren Wilkosz sat next to Assistant State's Attorney Robert Bastone in Interrogation Room D. Across the table from them, his hands neatly folded, sat Robin Gecht.

As long as Wilkosz was present at Area Five for the purpose of getting information about the Linda Sutton case, his turn to question Gecht further was kept on hold. But once Eddie Spreitzer had confessed, for himself and his boss, to the murder of Lorry Ann Borowski, positions shifted. Area Five had Spreitzer's confession, but they had no independent knowledge of the details of Lorry's disappearance to test the confession against. Wilkosz did. That Gecht and Spreitzer had killed Linda Sutton was something Wilkosz was sure of in his own mind, as were the Area Five detectives. But it was still supposition. They *knew* that the two men had killed Lorry Ann Borowski.

When a detective knows a suspect did it, and he has a confession to back it up, his business is to zero in and complete the investigation. Detectives' actions immediately following a confession will be scrutinized and dissected in minute detail later at trial. If a defense attorney can show that the detectives' actions following the confession were lackadaisical and disinterested, he will try to plant the suspicion in the jurors' minds that even the detectives didn't take the so-called confession seriously, and therefore it probably wasn't even true.

"Robin," Warren Wilkosz said, "I'm going to show you some photos. You tell me if you recognize any of the people in them."

Slowly, he spread photos of Linda Sutton, Lorry Ann Borowski, and other young women across the table between them. Robin Gecht leaned forward and studied the photos with great care, picking up and peering at each one before putting it back down and shaking his head.

Wilkosz, watching him carefully, was worried. By this time Eddie Spreitzer, who was still talking, had confessed to seven murders and one aggravated battery. He had named Robin Gecht as the impetus for each of the crimes. Gecht was a smooth and dangerous man, but Wilkosz knew that until they could

142

nail down provable details against him, they had nothing but a lot of talk.

"No," Gecht said. "I don't recognize any of them."

"Are you sure?"

"Positive. I never saw any of them women before." Gecht leaned back in his chair and shrugged, as if he, too, was sorry that he had been unable to help the police.

Wilkosz swept away the series of photos and began again to question Robin Gecht. He returned to certain questions that he had asked before, but now he phrased them differently. Gecht was very sharply focused, however, and he responded with the same calm certainty no matter how the questions were phrased.

As the interrogation continued, Wilkosz became fascinated with Robin Gecht's manipulative skills. Gecht, he saw, could react immediately to each nuance in the conversation. If Wilkosz seemed hostile, Gecht's attitude would become instantly submissive. When Wilkosz remained aloof and expressionless, Gecht would suddenly switch again, leaning forward and trying to recapture emotional contact.

"He first came across as if he was affronted," Wilkosz remembers, "saying that he was a businessman in good standing. He actually got quite huffy that he was being put through all this 'hassle'! Then he suddenly switched postures and acted like a frightened child. His voice was meek and he was eager to please. His big blue eyes were brimming with tears."

Wilkosz, trying to keep his own eyes and voice neutral, was amazed at Gecht's posturing. It was becoming more and more clear to him how easily Gecht would be able to control a stooge like Eddie Spreitzer. Even though Spreitzer was taller and bigger than Gecht, Wilkosz knew that it was often not the biggest but the craftiest, the psychologically strongest, dog that controlled the whole pack.

At one point in the questioning, Wilkosz felt that Robin Gecht's mannerisms became overtly homosexual. He flirted with Wilkosz, crossed and uncrossed his legs, and batted his eyelashes at the tall, attractive detective. When that failed to elicit any response, he moved on to the next pose, leaving that whole catalog of body language behind as if it had never existed.

By the time the interrogation was over, Gecht had taken on the role of "just one of the guys," talking casually with Wilkosz as though they were friends out for a drink together. This relaxed, almost happy manner may have been less the result of another calculated shift than because Robin Gecht probably was feeling genuine relief. He had gotten through the interrogation without once tripping himself up or admitting to anything.

After Wilkosz left the interrogation room, he sat at a spare desk in the squad room and got on the telephone with his office in Wheaton to keep his superiors apprised of his progress, or lack of it. Robin Gecht was allowed to rest alone for a while. Impatient as they were to keep the pressure on their prime catch, the detectives knew that such breaks in the action would carry great weight during the inevitable courtroom showdown with a defense team.

Area Five detectives Phil Murphy and Tom Flynn were still working their way, along with A.S.A. Beuke and the court reporter, through the muddled labyrinth of Eddie Spreitzer's memory. They came in and out of Interrogation Room F occasionally, getting coffee for themselves and Spreitzer, or asking one of the other detectives to check on some fact. Then Spreitzer was brought out of Room F in handcuffs and taken out of the building.

Two other veteran homicide detectives, Tim Nolan and Bob Doelker, were brought in to ask Robin Gecht about some of the murders that Spreitzer was confessing to. They didn't have much luck with Gecht either, but when they got to the subject of Sandra Delaware, Nolan asked Gecht if he had ever been in the area near or under the Fullerton Avenue bridge.

Gecht stroked his chin and looked upward, seeming to give the matter great thought. "I don't recall," he said. "I can't place the area. Perhaps if I saw it . . ."

Nolan and Doelker talked it over with Lieutenant Minogue and A.S.A. Bastone. They decided to take Robin for a ride to the Fullerton Avenue bridge. Along the way they stopped to get Gecht a hot dog and a cup of coffee.

While Warren Wilkosz and A.S.A. Bastone had been questioning Gecht about the DuPage County cases, Lieutenant Minogue had sent two of his men off with Eddie Spreitzer to Schiller Woods so that Eddie could show the detectives where, he claimed, he and Robin had dumped the body of a still unknown black prostitute.

At the huge Schiller Woods Forest Preserve complex, Eddie directed the detectives onto Irving Park Road, and west to the second entrance into the preserve. He showed the detectives the turnaround where he said Robin had parked a borrowed yellow station wagon they'd been using that night. Eddie led the detectives up an incline into the heavily forested woods.

After only a few yards, however, Eddie swung around and told the detectives that he was confused. "I can't remember which way we went," he said.

Then he described for the detectives what he

did remember, looking up through the twisted, ghostly branches and seeing the moon, "all weird and spooky, you know," he said, "while Robin was beating her head in with a baseball bat." His description of the moment sounded like a scene from Poe or Stephen King, though somewhat less articulate, and the detectives recall that Eddie was "freaked" just remembering those rattling black branches and "the wind and the moon and all that stuff." Given Eddie's limited brain power and his and Gecht's ghoulish purpose, it is not surprising that such a scene would spook him, though he seemed less bothered about taking part in a brutal murder than he did about ghosts and goblins.

It had been over a year ago, he explained to the detectives, and it had been in the middle of the night. The trees had been in full foliage when he and Robin had brought the girl in, and now most of the branches were bare.

"Keep looking," the detectives told him. He shuffled along and they trudged after him. But after a few minutes they could see it was no use. Eddie was lost.

Next, the detectives took Eddie to LaBagh Woods, to the scene of another alleged murder. It was the same story there. Eddie had no hesitation showing the detectives to an entrance into the preserve, and showing them where Robin had driven over a curb and parked the red Dodge van. But as soon as he and the detectives entered the woods, he became lost. The detectives took Eddie back to the squad car and headed for their next stop, the Fullerton Avenue bridge, site of Sandra Delaware's death, where police department divers still hadn't found a knife in the murky water.

When Nolan and Doelker showed up with Robin Gecht, Eddie Spreitzer already was down on the embankment, pointing out to his detectives exactly where he and Gecht had driven alongside the bridge and exactly where they'd killed Sandra Delaware.

Nolan and Doelker watched Gecht's face as he stared down at Eddie Spreitzer, but Gecht was well aware he was being watched, and his face was carefully blank. He showed no expression at all.

"This area look familiar, Robin?"

"No," Gecht said, "I've never been here before."

They drove him back to Area Five and put him back in Room D. A short time later Eddie, too, was brought back to Area Five, back to Room F, and the detectives all gathered to decide what their next step should be. They knew that the news-hungry crowd gathering downstairs, and the pointed questions from downtown, couldn't be put off much longer.

Chapter Seventeen

By this time, details of the Gecht case had
worked their way through the chain of police
command. Every reporter in town knew
about it. Calls were coming in from downtown, from the deputy chiefs at Police Headquarters. The superintendent had been told
about the Spreitzer confessions. Mayor Jane
Byrne had been told. Both were still inun-
dated in the flood of Tylenol-related news,
but both asked to be notified, even at home,
of any major developments.

Downstairs at Area Five, reporters demanded an updated statement. The tele-
phones rang incessantly. The local Chicago
TV stations, always fiercely competitive,
clamored for details. At one point so many
reporters and camera crews had gathered at
the 25th District desk that Lieutenant Minogue had to post a guard on the stairway
leading up to the Detective Division.

"Reporters tended to lose their hearing

when they were asked to wait downstairs," Lieutenant Minogue says. "Somehow, they kept turning up, wandering into the Detective squad room, asking questions, listening in on conversations, trying to browse through the preliminary reports."

Reporters and police officers, particularly detectives, have a unique and somewhat symbiotic relationship in Chicago. The average street police officer tends to look upon reporters as one of the lowest forms of life, only a layer above lawyers. The mistrust is perhaps not without reason. Fairness, and sometimes even truth, often go out the window when a good story comes in the door.

But there is another side to the police/reporter relationship. Sometimes a police officer wants to get something into print, maybe something the Department doesn't officially want to get out. Many police officers, and especially detectives, have one newspaper or television reporter who has earned their respect and trust. They will give a story to that one reporter and no one else.

On the day of Eddie Spreitzer's confessions, the relationship between the police and the press was, at least temporarily, adversarial. A barricade was set up across the doors to keep reporters from wandering in and out while the detectives continued their investigation.

One reason that things were especially tense between the police and the press at this time was that a few weeks earlier a local television reporter had been allowed to hang around in Area Five while he waited for a particular detective. The reporter was there to ask questions about a case that had been getting a lot of coverage, but which the de tectives had been reluctant to discuss fully. On that case, the detectives felt they wanted to sit on their information until they had fully developed their case, and the reporters felt they were being blindsided and misled.

While the reporter was waiting, he "happened to notice" a detective's red spiral notebook lying on the desk. The notebook was filled with jottings containing some startling names and information. Thinking he had found an exclusive scoop on the case he was following, the reporter rushed back to his TV studio and convinced his superiors that he had the night's lead story. The story, with the reporter's "exclusive, inside information," was splashed all over the TV newscasts that evening. And then all hell broke loose.

The Chicago chief of detectives called the TV station to let them know that the juicy tidbits being reported were, in fact, about another case. The police were enraged that details of one of their developing cases had been stolen and misreported. The reporters, in turn, were enraged, convinced that the red spiral notebook had been deliberately left out to mislead the reporter. Whatever the case, the incident had left a bad taste in everyone's mouth, and everybody working on the Gecht case wanted to make sure there was not another fiasco.

Chapter Eighteen

"I told them about all the girls," Eddie said. He stood, tense as a trip wire, in Interrogation Room D, facing the man who police believed had worked Eddie like a puppet.

Lieutenant Minogue and two detectives stood behind Spreitzer. Gecht sat at a table. Minogue watched both Eddie and Gecht. Minogue and the others had decided to bring the two men together, thinking that Gecht might open up if he was confronted with Eddie's confessions face to face.

Everybody waited for Gecht to respond. Most anxious, perhaps, was Eddie Spreitzer, who stood trembling, mouth open, terrified. Gecht, sitting calmly at the table, was expressionless. Finally, Eddie spoke again. "Robin, I said I told them about the girls."

Robin Gecht looked up at Eddie for a long moment. A little smile played around his lips. "I have no idea what you're talking about." Then he looked back down, seeming to study his fingernails.

After the detectives took a shaken Eddie Spreitzer back to Room F, they watched him through the viewing window. He began to cry. Then he became extremely agitated. He picked at his nails and chewed his lip and scratched himself, all the while sobbing.

Suddenly, Eddie called out that he wanted to "see the boss."

Lieutenant Minogue went in to see him.

By this time Minogue had spent some time interviewing Gecht, an unusual step, because Minogue didn't like to interfere with his detectives' investigations. But the lieutenant had been anxious to get a firsthand impression of the man who was causing such an uproar. Minogue had spent less than a half hour with Gecht and had not questioned him about the crimes. That was his detectives' job. He had simply asked Gecht about himself and talked for a while. But Minogue still had his street smarts and without even having mentioned any of the murders, he came away from Gecht, telling one of his men, "That man is an actor. And he's evil, icy, pure evil."

Now, as Minogue stood in front of Eddie Spreitzer, with his men watching from the door, he hoped this was a break that would help his men put Gecht away.

"What can I do for you?" Minogue asked.

"I want to change my statement," Eddie cried.

"Change it? Why?"

"Because," Eddie said, "it wasn't me and Robin that did all the stuff I told you."

"I see," Minogue said. He had heard this song many times before. In fact, he and his men had been expecting this. Once Eddie realized how tightly he'd drawn the noose around his own neck, he would try to back out by concocting some new story about how he hadn't really been there, after all. But Spreitzer surprised him.

"Well, Eddie, if it wasn't you and Robin, who was it?"

"It was me and Andy."

Long seconds went by. The stunned cops tried to assimilate what they'd just heard. Andy? Who the hell was Andy?

Minogue stepped into Room F and sat down. "Tell us about Andy."

"He's a guy me and Robin hang out with sometimes," Eddie said.

"What's Andy's last name, Eddie?"

"I don't know."

"You don't know."

"I know it starts with a K," Eddie said. "It's a long name, foreign-like, and it starts with a K. He's my girlfriend's brother."

"He's your girlfriend's brother and you

don't know his last name? What's your girl-friend's last name?"

The sarcasm was lost on Eddie. "It's the same as Andy's," he said. "It starts with a K just like his does. But it's too long, and I can never remember it."

"Where does Andy live?"

"On North Avenue out in Villa Park, right near Winchell's Donut Shop."

"The address, Eddie."

"I don't know it, I swear," Eddie said. "But I could take you there to the apartment."

"We couldn't believe what we were hear-ing," Wilkosz said later. "Was there a *third* member in this unholy alliance? What about the seventy-eight-page statement that Eddie had just given that morning?"

Wilkosz and Flynn went to Room D, where Flynn asked Robin Gecht who Andy was. Robin thought for a moment, and said the only Andy he knew was Andy Kokoraleis, a young man who had baby-sat for him from time to time. He'd met Andy, he said, while he was doing some electrical work on the apartment complex along North Avenue. Gecht said that was all he knew of anybody named Andy. He failed to point out, as detec-tives were to find out shortly, that he and Andy had been next-door neighbors at the time, or that Andy had later come to live with him in Chicago at the house on McVickers.

As the men walked out of the room, Wilkosz repeated the name several times.

"Don't tell me you know this Andy," Flynn asked, astonished.

"Yes, I do. I know Andy Kokoraleis quite well. Him and his brother Tom. Andy's one of those wild-ass teenagers who's always in trouble. Minor stuff mostly, breaking bottles on a street corner, harassing passersby, that kind of thing."

The men walked out into the squad room, where Wilkosz told the Area Five guys about the Kokoraleis family. The mother had died years ago, and the six Kokoraleis kids were being raised by their father, an old country Greek butcher who worked long hours and couldn't seem to control his teenage children. The kids were on the streets at all hours. They were well-known to the local Villa Park police and to the DuPage County Sheriff's Department.

Wilkosz recalled that Andy's younger sister, *Elizabeth, had filed several complaints with the youth protection agency. She said her father had sexually molested her. The way her father told it, she was just rebelling against his authority. She had been taken out of the home. Later, Elizabeth recanted her charges and was returned to the home, only to run away. The Kokoraleis kids, Wilkosz said, belonged to a troubled, and trouble-some, family.

During the short time it had taken Flynn and Wilkosz to question Robin about Andy, Eddie Spreitzer had revised his story a number of times. Now he was telling Minogue and Nolan and Doelker that he had never been at any of the crime scenes. He had only heard Andy and Robin discuss the incidents.

"I see," Lieutenant Minogue said. Then he read to Eddie his description, on page 25 of his statement, of how he'd stabbed Sandra Delaware two or three times.

"Was that a lie, Eddie?"

"Yes," Spreitzer said, "that was a lie."

"But why would you lie?"

"I was afraid."

"What about the guys you described in the shooting on North Avenue, Eddie? How did you know that a .22 rifle and a .38 pistol were used if you weren't there?"

Eddie replied that he had heard Robin and Andy talking about going out to "shoot some niggers." He said he brought the rifle out to the van for them, but didn't go along. This was blatant nonsense and the detectives knew it. Eddie's previous description of where the victims had been standing by the telephone booth, and how each man had fallen, had been right on the money.

Eddie's statement continued, but none of it made much sense. He changed back to the story that he and Andy had committed the murders, not Robin. For Wilkosz and the others, interviewing Eddie Spreitzer was like trying to grab a handful of fog.

When they asked Eddie about all the black prostitutes whose murders he had so vividly described, he said he was there. Then he wasn't there. Then it was he and Andy. Then it was Andy and Robin, but not him. He rambled on, concocting first one version and then another of the various crimes, and was unable to come up with specific locations or details for any of them.

The detectives backed off for a bit, letting Eddie have coffee and a cigarette. Then Wilkosz, who was by now accepted as a full member of the detective team, sat down with Eddie and asked him about Linda Sutton.

Eddie said he and Andy Kokoraleis had killed her back in May 1981 at some construction site, severed her breasts, and then driven around with her in Eddie's car until they dumped her in the field behind the Moonlit Motel.

"So it was you and Robin that killed Linda Sutton? Who was driving the van when you picked her up?"

"Robin was."

"What about Andy? Was he there, too?"

Eddie suddenly realized that he'd been tricked. "No, I was wrong," he stammered. "It wasn't Robin. It was me and Andy, like I said."

Eddie stammered again, and the detectives realized that having taken Eddie into Room D to confront Gecht, they had triggered a very different reaction from the one they'd been looking for. Gecht hadn't broken at all, but Spreitzer had broken down even further. He was so afraid of what Robin was capable of doing to him for confessing that he was now babbling in circles, trying to get Gecht out of it. Apparently, the dim lights inside Eddie's head didn't have enough wattage to realize that Robin Gecht was never going to run into Eddie out on the streets again, because Eddie was never going to be out there again.

Eddie went back to describing the Linda Sutton murder again, without Robin again, and he offered an explanation of why he was getting his facts confused.

"I keep getting that one mixed up with the other one, the lady with the pointy eyes and yellow skin."

"The what?" Detective Nolan gasped. Warren Wilkosz, who had been doodling on his notepad, suddenly sat up and looked at Spreitzer with narrowed eyes.

Nolan looked at Wilkosz, wondering at his

Linda Sutton was probably the first victim
of the Ripper gang. Her mutilated remains
were found behind a suburban motel.
(*Inside Detective* magazine)

Linda Sutton's murder behind the Brer Rabbit Motel
remained unsolved for a year and a half.
(Jaye Slade Fletcher)

"Robin Gecht just looked at you and told you
to do a thing, and you had to do it,"
according to one of his followers.
(*Inside Detective* magazine)

Vivacious, popular Rose Beck Davis was murdered in a gangway just off Chicago's luxurious Lake Shore Drive. (Denise Harnish)

A special bulletin was issued following Shui Mak's disappearance. Not a single clue ever turned up. Her skeletal remains were discovered at a construction site six months later.

Missing

SHUI MAK was last seen on May 29, 1982, walking along the roadway in Hanover Park, Illinois. Investigation by the DuPage County Sheriff's Department disclosed that Mak's absence does not appear to have been planned. Foul play is suspected.

MISSING

LORRY BOROWSKI

**AGE·21 HT. 5´3˝ WT. 129 HAIR·LT. BROWN
EYES· BLUE**   Last seen at 8:15 AM SAT.
**5·15·82 IN THE PARKING LOT OF THE
SHOPPING CENTER AT RT. 83 & ST. CHARLES
ROAD IN ELMHURST.** Wearing green khaki slacks
& white blouse, carrying white purse. **CONTACT
ELMHURST POLICE ~ 530-3050** gr
Illinois Area Code 312

Lorrry Borowski's parents created this flier, which
was widely circulated in the Chicago area, asking
for help in finding their missing daughter.

Detective Warren Wilkosz knew that whatever
criminal activity Robin Gecht was involved in,
Eddie Spreitzer was involved in, too.
(Jaye Slade Fletcher)

Eddie Spreitzer broke the Ripper case
wide open when he implicated himself and
the others in a string of grisly murders.
(*Inside Detective* magazine)

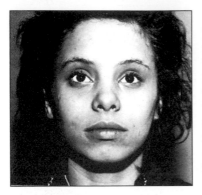

Nineteen-year-old Sandra Delaware was "the girl under the bridge." Spreitzer said the knife they used to kill her was thrown into the Chicage River. It has never been recovered. (*Inside Detective* magazine)

Cook County Assistant States Attorney Bob Bastone directed the detectives during the long weekend of horrifying confessions. (William T. McDermott)

Tommy Kokoraleis helped send his brother to Death Row when he confessed that the gang had cannibalized their victims. (*Inside Detective* magazine)

The Cook County Criminal Courts Building, where Robin Gecht, Eddie Spreitzer, and Andy Kokoraleis were sentenced. (William T. McDermott)

Andy Kokoraleis "blazed threat" across the courtroom at Prosecutor Telander. "Andy was an enjoyer," Telander said. "Andy did what he did because he liked it." (*Inside Detective* magazine)

It took the jury just an hour to sentence Andy Kokorleis to Death Row. (Rosalie Morris)

reaction. "You know who he's talking about?"

Wilkosz nodded and closed his eyes, sighing heavily. "Yes, unfortunately, I think I do. Good God, will this ever end?"

"What about the lady with the pointy eyes, Eddie?" Nolan asked.

But Eddie Spreitzer leaned forward and started retching, saying only that she'd hitchhiked a ride with him, Andy, and Robin, and they all had driven around drinking beer. He said that "her tits were too small" and that he cut her. Then Eddie shut up. Turning his face away, he stared at the wall and refused to say anything else. Obviously, something about this particular case was so awful that even Eddie Spreitzer was having trouble talking about his part in it. The detectives looked at each other and nodded. They would try switching cases.

"Okay, Eddie," said Detective Nolan, "let's talk about Lorraine Borowski some more."

Eddie went off into a disjointed account of how he'd been driving around by himself, "somewhere west of Chicago," and had seen a girl sitting on a bench. He picked her up and they drove around and had some beers. Then they parked, and when she wasn't looking, he stuck a knife in his boot. They drove around some more and then parked and talked for a while, and then she wanted to walk. As they were walking along, Eddie said, he pulled the knife and stabbed her. Then he cut off her breasts and drove away. Later, he said, he drove into an alley and cut the breasts into small pieces and threw them into a garbage can.

"Where were you driving when you spotted her, Eddie?"

"I don't know."

"What kind of bench was she sitting on?"

"I don't know."

"Where did you walk? Where did you park? Where did you stab her?"

"I don't know," Eddie said.

Finally, the detectives broke off the questioning. They were getting nowhere. It was clear that, after coming face to face with Robin Gecht, Eddie was simply making up whatever came into his head. He was lying, and badly. It was time to break off the questioning for the night. A couch was brought in from the second-floor women's lounge and put into Interrogation Room F. The lights were turned off and Eddie was allowed to sleep.

Chapter Nineteen

Late that evening attorney Julius Eccles swept into the squad room and was taken to his client, Robin Gecht. Eccles was well known in Chicago for his flamboyance and for his tendency to take on high-profile cases. After a few minutes he came out and conferred with the detectives. Then he went back in and told Gecht, "You're going to be charged with the Area Six case. Either I or one of my associates will be at the arraignment."

Then he swept out again. Neither he nor any of his associates ever made another appearance in behalf of Robin Gecht. The attorney-client privilege is sacrosanct, so one can only speculate that either money was an issue, or perhaps the true nature of the crimes attributed to Robin Gecht dampened any showboat enthusiasm.

A short time later, a detective and two uniformed officers came into Interrogation

Room D. The detective told Gecht that he was going to be formally charged with attempted murder in the Area Six case. The uniformed officers cuffed him and escorted him to a squadrol, commonly known as a paddy wagon.

After Robin Gecht was taken to Area Six, he was read the Miranda warnings and formally charged with attempted murder in connection with the October 31 attack on Cynthia Smith. While Area Six was not at all happy with Smith's story, she was sticking to it, insisting that Robin Gecht was the man who had inflicted her injuries. Gecht was taken downstairs to the lockup to be finger-printed and photographed. After processing, he was taken back up to a detective inter-view room, where he would remain until his appearance before a judge on Monday morning.

Usually, a prisoner stays in the lockup, not in a detective interrogation room, while awaiting his court appearance. But Robin Gecht was an unusual prisoner. Detectives were determined not to take any chances with Gecht's health and safety. He was going to live with them, right in the detective squad room, until they could deliver him safely to court.

While Spreitzer at Area Five and Gecht at Area Six slept, Wilkosz and the other detectives connected to the case did not. Everyone was pulling out reports and comparing details, or on the phone ordering back copies. Wilkosz was on the telephone constantly with his superiors at the DuPage County Sheriff's Office in Wheaton, advising them of developments at Area Five and requesting that various reports be pulled up and made available to him, including, just in case, the numerous police reports about the Kokoraleis family.

By this time Wilkosz was compelled to learn as much as possible about Gecht and Spreitzer. He wanted to know about all the murders, not just the ones on his turf. And he particularly wanted to know about "the lady with the pointy eyes and yellow skin" that Eddie Spreitzer had mentioned and then refused to talk any more about. Eddie had described her as a young woman who willingly had gotten into their car and shared some beers with them as they cruised around. Sure, Eddie, Wilkosz thought as he asked the information operator for the telephone number of the Cook County Sheriff's Homicide Division in Skokie.

"Detective Larry Troka, please. Larry? Warren Wilkosz here. I'm in Chicago, at Area Five. Yeah, that's right, the hooker killers. Larry, one of them is talking about having

killed an Oriental woman, out in the suburbs. No details yet, but we'll get to it. I was
wondering about the name of that missing
Chinese girl you handled last spring—you
found her skeleton a couple months ago in
Barrington."

Wilkosz hung up the phone, tapping his
pen on the desktop, and wondering to himself exactly how Shui Mak had met her
death. Even Eddie Spreitzer, who had recounted the most mind-numbing horrors
with little show of conscience, didn't want to
talk about what they'd done to Shui Mak.

Chapter Twenty

It was 11:00 P.M., May 29, 1982. The Mak family, recent Chinese immigrants, closed their suburban restaurant, Ling-Ling's. The entire family worked there and now everyone worked to clean up the kitchen. They all worked long hours, the parents, the children, the uncle, and the grandparents, but it was worth it; this was America, at last, and they were free.

They were a happy family, but on this particular night there was distress. Mrs. Mak was troubled because her son, Kent, and her daughter Shui had been arguing all evening. The reason: another sister had decided to marry an American man. Kent was against the marriage, Shui was all for it.

At 1:30 A.M., Shui, slim, pretty, thirty years old, got into her brother Kent's car. They headed west on Irving Park Road toward home. Shui's parents and sister followed in another car. Without their mother there to intervene, Shui and her brother argued even more vociferously about the impending wedding. Kent was adamant. This marriage flew in the face of thousands of years of arranged marriages, and it was wrong. Shui felt just as strongly: this was America, a woman had the right to marry the man she loved; it was romantic, it was brave.

"They are in love," Shui argued, "that's all that matters. It does not matter that he is not Chinese; he is a good, kind man and she will be happy." Shui was perhaps thinking of her own impending appointment to meet the young Chinese man her parents had already picked out for her. "This is America, things are different here."

Soon brother and sister were shouting at each other. Kent's temper finally got the better of him. At a red light he pulled over to the side of the road and ordered Shui to get out of his car. She could ride with their parents. Kent was unaware that his parents, thinking he had car trouble, had gone ahead of him and pulled over.

Shui climbed out of her brother's car. The light changed and Kent drove off. His parents up ahead, seeing that the car was all right, followed. Shui was alone on the side of the road. When she finally realized that her parents had driven off without her, she began to walk. Ahead she saw a Denny's all-night restaurant. She walked toward it. A squad car, driving in the other direction, slowed, then made a U-turn and cruised up next to the girl. "You okay?" asked the lone patrolman. Shui smiled shyly and nodded. "Fine," she said. She pointed at the restaurant, which was less than a block ahead. The patrolman nodded, waved, and drove off into the night.

Later, that patrolman wept when he heard what had happened. "How could I have known?" he tormented himself. "Thousands of Oriental families have moved into the western suburbs over the last decade or so, sponsored by some of our churches through the international sanctuary movement. They're good, law-abiding people and they take care of their own problems, rarely coming to the police for anything. If that had been an American-born woman walking alone out there in the dark, she probably would have accepted a lift from a marked squad car, but a newly arrived Chinese woman? Never. I don't know what else I could have done, but that night will haunt me all my life."

Moments after the squad car disappeared, a red van slowed down and began keeping pace alongside Shui. She glanced over quickly and then continued walking. She pulled her red sweater more tightly around her, trying to ignore the comments from the men in the van. She grasped her long gold neck chain with its jade heart. She had brought it from China with her, and it had always brought her good luck.

The men in the van continued to talk to her, though she wasn't sure what they were saying. Shui had only been in America for three years, and her English was just passable. Shui admired all things American, but she still was uncomfortable with the easy familiarity with which young American men and women approached each other. She found it embarrassing and humiliating, and could not yet bring herself to speak socially with any man who had not been introduced to her by her family. Shui put her head down, quickened her pace, and did her best to ignore the young men cruising alongside her.

Suddenly, the van sped up and veered over sharply in front of her. The rear doors flew open and two young men leaped out. Shui jumped back. She tried to run. But they grabbed her. They flung her into the van, facedown on the floor. Then they jumped in and slammed the rear doors. The van peeled out onto the highway. Shui, her mind spinning, trying to understand what was happening, raised herself up. "Please," she cried, "please."

One of the men grabbed her by her shirtfront and pulled her to her feet. As she looked at his thick lips and wild red hair, Shui began to sob, then to scream. Holding her up by her sweater, the young man hauled back and punched her full in the mouth. Shui shrieked. Then he punched her again, and again and again. Finally she went limp, and he threw her to the floor again.

Now two men prodded and poked Shui's limp form until they had her face-up on the floor. A flashlight flicked on and they inspected her battered face.

The red-haired man who had beaten Shui now stared down at her. His forehead wrinkled in confusion. "She's funny-looking, Andy," he said, his voice whining in disappointment. "Her eyes are pointy and her skin's all yellow or something." He seemed befuddled.

The other man pushed him aside and stared down at her.

"It's a chink!" he said. "We got ourselves a fucking chink this time!" He kicked Shui in the side, but she didn't move.

Twenty minutes later, the van pulled off the highway. Then it bounced through a weedy field and along a bumpy pathway, and came to a stop. There came three hard knocks on the partition.

Eddie and Andy knew the signal—they'd done this many times before. The two young men jumped from the back of the van, carrying the now moaning woman with them. They propped her up against the side of the van and waited as their leader came out from the driver's seat and walked around to the back.

They stood, silent, as he walked back and forth inspecting Shui. "Let's see what we got here."

Eddie jumped and began tearing Shui's blouse and bra. She was regaining consciousness and she flailed ineffectually at the hands on her body. The three men looked her over.

"Jesus Christ," the leader screamed. "She's got no tits at all!"

Eddie, already upset and confused over this one, leaped forward and grabbed Shui by the hair. He spun her around and smashed the back of her head into the side of the van, over and over again. He howled in frustration. He didn't like to disappoint the boss. Finally, he let go of Shui's hair and she dropped to the ground.

"It's okay," Robin Gecht said. He patted Eddie on the arm. "It's okay. We can do this anyway. Bring the knives."

Chapter Twenty-one

Late on Sunday morning, Chicago Police Superintendent Richard J. Brzeczek (Bree-zek) arrived at Area Five. Several chiefs and an assistant deputy superintendent were already there, overseeing what had become an enormously complex investigation. Brzeczek had been on the phone late into the night talking with Lieutenant John Minogue.

"Spreitzer is telling a dozen different stories," Minogue had said. "Gecht denies everything. Now Spreitzer says there was a third guy involved. We're on the way out to pick him up."

Regardless of who was involved, Brzeczek knew that these were not ordinary crimes. They were particularly monstrous. And the press wanted answers.

As Brzeczek and his driver passed through the front doors of the building, camera lights came on, flashbulbs popped, TV and newspaper reporters surrounded him. The press was always glad to see Brzeczek. He was a man they could talk to. Brzeczek enjoyed an excellent reputation with the Chicago media. He had a sharp, biting wit and thrived on the verbal sparring sessions with the reporters. He was respected by most news organizations as an open-minded, pro-active thinker—unusual qualities in a profession that tends to breed paranoia and an us-versus-them mentality. If the media exposed problems and inadequacies in the Department, he listened, acknowledged the point, and set about dealing with the problem.

Just thirty-eight years old when Mayor Jane Byrne appointed him superintendent of the fourteen-thousand-man force in January 1980, Brzeczek was the youngest superintendent in Chicago's history and, many would say, the most brilliant. An attorney, he had graduated first in his class from the prestigious John Marshall Law School, and had scored first in every promotional exam within the Police Department.

While he had the respect of the media and the admiration of the public, Brzeczek's standing with the rank-and-file members of his department was considerably more mixed. He had only "worked the street" for a couple of years as a young police officer before he began to move up the ranks in various administrative positions. Many of the district officers re-

sented that their boss was not a "cop's cop."
To them he was a glorified corporate lawyer in
a classy three-piece suit. A lot of police officers
felt that Brzeczek was arrogant and snobbish,
and that he looked down on them. Brilliant as
he was, Brzeczek was not good as a "people
person." On a large scale he could be a daz-
zling administrator, but on a one-to-one basis
he often offended and insulted people at many
levels of the huge department, and rumbles
about their "kiddie-cop" boss reverberated in
the outlying districts.

As the reporters at Area Five surrounded
him, Brzeczek explained that his comments
would have to be brief. He did not yet have
all the details of the investigation's progress,
and he was here at Area Five to do just that,
to gather information.

"We've heard rumors of a Satan-worshiping
cult and horrible mutilations," one reporter
said. "Is it true?"

Brzeczek again said he couldn't give out
any details, because he didn't have them yet.
He promised to hold a full-scale press conference as soon as he had all the facts. Then
he excused himself and went up the stairs
and past the barricades.

From his numerous phone conversations
with Lieutenant Minogue, Brzeczek, of course,
knew a lot more about the investigation than
he indicated to the reporters. But he was a

lawyer, and until formal charges were filed, he was not going to give out details of what were still unsubstantiated claims.

Brzeczek sat down in the Area Five watch commander's office with the assistant state's attorney, Lieutenant Minogue, the deputy chiefs from Police Headquarters, and the detectives who'd been talking with Eddie Spreitzer and Robin Gecht. Point by point Minogue and the detectives went over everything they had. Brzeczek, possessed of a phenomenal memory and proud of it, did not need to take notes. He would remember every word. A fastidious man, Brzeczek felt physically sickened at what he was hearing. Several times he shook his head and shuddered with disgust.

"The only physical evidence we've got so far," Minogue explained, "are the three knives we took from the back of Gecht's van. The carpeting in the rear of the van appears to have been changed recently, and damp spots under it show the floor has recently been washed. Detective Herigodt found an eight-inch knife with a serrated blade in a plastic bucket just inside the van's rear doors. It matches exactly the knife Eddie Spreitzer described."

Minogue told Brzeczek that traces of what appeared to be dried blood had been found on the blade. All three knives had been sent to the crime lab for analysis.

The conference went on for hours. Each detective talked about what he knew and what he thought. When Brzeczek had absorbed enough information he gave his orders:

"I want a search of LaBagh Woods."

He knew there was little chance of finding anything in the huge forest preserve, but maybe they'd get lucky. Even if they didn't, the search would keep the TV cameras busy for the afternoon, which was exactly what Brzeczek wanted. He ordered that two detective teams be borrowed from each of the city's six areas and that they all meet at three o'clock that afternoon at LaBagh Woods, under the supervision of Lieutenant Minogue.

At the same time several teams of Area Five detectives would head out to Villa Park to meet up with Warren Wilkosz and other DuPage sheriff's detectives, where they would attempt to pick up Andy Kokoraleis for questioning. Brzeczek warned the men not to take any chances in taking Kokoraleis into custody. They didn't know yet what kind of man he was, but if he'd done the things Eddie Spreitzer was accusing him of, he was very dangerous, indeed.

Brzeczek had gotten his information and given his instructions. It was time to leave. He ordered his driver to take his car around to the back of the building, into the police-restricted lot. Then he left by the back stairway, avoiding the reporters who were still clustered around the front door.

From his car phone, Brzeczek called Kathy Kajari, his director of news affairs, and told her to announce over the City News wire that there would be a search for bodies in LaBagh Woods. It was a certainty that no news crew in town would take the chance of missing out on the search. Just in case bodies were discovered, the dramatic footage of cops carrying body bags out of the woods was too good to pass up. They would all be there.

At three that afternoon, two dozen extremely unhappy detectives stood milling about in the parking turnaround at LaBagh Woods. It was cold out and misty, with the wind whipping around them. Despite the weather, most of them had been called out of their offices, and they wore the detectives' standard work clothes: sports coat, dress slacks, and loafers. They groaned when TV camera trucks began pulling into the lot.

For hours the twenty-four detectives, in pairs, searched through soggy mounds of wet brush and dead leaves. When darkness began to settle in the woods they straggled out, some sniffling and coughing, most blistering the air with curses. Their booty for the day: a few dozen empty beer cans and some styrofoam packaging from McDonald's.

Chapter Twenty-two

While two dozen wet detectives were losing their sense of humor in the LaBagh Woods, Detective Flynn was making progress along with Warren Wilkosz and DuPage County Sheriff's detectives and a squad car from the Villa Park Police Department.

"It's standard police procedure to have a marked squad along on a raid or other type of plainclothes operation," Wilkosz explains. "It wouldn't do to have someone mistake the armed plainclothesmen for armed robbers or home invaders."

Eddie Spreitzer, sitting in the backseat of the squad car, led the detectives to the Kokoraleis town house in the Anzak buildings. The eighteen buildings, named after the man who had constructed them, stood in a long row along the 800 and 900 blocks of West North Avenue in Villa Park. The buildings were set in facing pairs across small patches of grass, and each contained six town houses. Many of the buildings had fallen into disrepair. Some had cardboard tacked up over broken windows. Electrical extension cords hung like clotheslines from one open upstairs window, across the sidewalk, and into another window. Wilkosz had been inside these town houses many times, and he knew that they were all alike, with a tiny living room and kitchen on the first floor and two small bedrooms and a minuscule bath upstairs. The town houses were extremely cramped, but rents were cheap and leases weren't required. The Villa Park police had visited the complex often because the rear parking lot of the buildings had become a hangout for teenagers drinking beer or smoking pot.

When all the cars had pulled up, the detectives, their guns held at their sides, moved cautiously toward the Kokoraleis town house. Flynn approached the door. On either side of him, out of sight of anyone in the house, were two backup teams of detectives. Flynn rapped twice. He waited. The door was opened by a thin, slightly built, pleasant-looking young man with long brown hair that fell to his shoulders. Flynn identified himself and asked for Andrew Kokoraleis.

"I'm Andy Kokoraleis," the young man said.

"Andy, we'd like you to come with us to Area Five police headquarters."

"Oh," Andy said. Then, "What for?"

"We want to talk to you about some friends of yours, Eddie Spreitzer and Robin Gecht."

"Okay," Andy said. He didn't look surprised. "I'll go with you."

Kokoraleis went back inside and got a jacket, while detectives watched him. He was alone.

By the time Andy was settled in a squad car, Eddie Spreitzer was already being driven back to Area Five. The two men did not see each other.

An hour later, Detective Flynn, who by this time was as obsessed with the case as Wilkosz was, began the questioning of Andy Kokoraleis in Interview Room E, between Robin's and Eddie's rooms.

"Andy," Flynn said. He handed the young man a cup of coffee and sat down across from him. "This is pretty serious stuff, what we want to talk to you about. Your pal Eddie Spreitzer has implicated you in a series of murders."

Andy looked at him. "You mean all eighteen of them?" he asked.

Jesus, Flynn thought. Eighteen! Stay calm, he told himself, don't get excited. He didn't want Andy to know that he didn't know about all eighteen.

"You remember that there were eighteen?" he said.

Andy hung his head and nodded. "Yes."

"Why?"

"Because ever since this thing started, I've dreamt about them every single night."

"I'm sure it's been tough on you," Flynn said. "Tell me, Andy, do you remember one of the women being an Oriental girl?"

Andy nodded.

"Tell me what happened to her, Andy."

As Andy Kokoraleis began to tell his terrible tale, the detectives could see that he was far more lucid than Eddie had been, and far more in control of himself. Flynn could see that Andy was scared, that he knew he was in very big trouble, but he didn't have the edge-of-hysteria mannerisms that Eddie had displayed.

Andy told the detectives that he, Eddie Spreitzer, and Robin Gecht had been driving around early one morning in May. They were in Robin's van and Robin was driving. Then, near Route 19 and Barrington Road, they spotted an Oriental girl walking along the side of the road. Robin pulled over and told Andy to get out and see if he could talk the girl into getting in with them.

"I could hardly understand her," Andy told

Flynn, "but it was obvious she did not want to get into the van."

Andy said he had looked at Robin and shaken his head. Robin then tapped his foot twice on the floor, and Eddie jumped out of the back. Eddie and Andy grabbed the girl, who was screaming, and dragged her into the rear of the van.

"She kept screaming so I punched her in the face as hard as I could," Andy said. "Eddie and I took turns punching her. When she finally fell on the floor I put the hand-cuffs on her."

They drove for some time, and when they stopped, they were at a construction site. As Andy described the location, Flynn recognized it from Eddie Spreitzer's description.

"When we dragged the girl out of the van, she woke up and started screaming again," Andy said, "so I punched her in the face. Then Robin pushed me aside and he punched her in the face until she fell to the ground. Robin dragged her over to some bushes and wrapped wire around her throat."

It was then, Andy said, that Robin began cutting the girl while Eddie held the wire around her throat. Each of the men took turns inserting themselves in the wound, first Robin, then Eddie, and then Andy.

"When we were finished, Robin dragged her into the bushes, and we left."

These stories were hard to take, even for thick-skinned cops. Flynn took a deep breath. He drank some of his coffee and tried to push down the sickening feeling that had been gaining on him during the past twenty-four hours. He asked Andy about Sandra Delaware.

"Who's that?" Andy asked.

"The girl under the bridge," Flynn said.

Andy's version of the Delaware murder differed somewhat from Eddie's, but his made more sense, given the condition of Sandra's body.

As Andy told it, they had picked the girl up and driven to the spot under the bridge. There they threw her out of the van and forcibly stripped her.

"Robin fucked her while she blew Eddie. When she started screaming I picked up a rock and shoved it into her mouth. I tied my bandanna around her face. Then I picked up an old wine bottle and told her to sit on it. When she wouldn't do it, Eddie got mad and he stabbed her. Then I grabbed the knife and I stabbed her, too."

As she fell to her knees, Andy said, he forced the wine bottle under her and then pushed her down on it. This explained the large pool of blood under her buttocks when her body was found. When they were finished, Eddie threw the knife and the bottle into the Chicago River.

The detectives sat awhile with Andy, asking details of one case or another, comparing what he said against Eddie Spreitzer's version of events. Like Eddie, Andy would get the details of one murder mixed up with another, then have to go back and correct them. The detectives could see he was getting tired and confused.

Then Andy mentioned a woman they'd grabbed "off Rush Street" just two months ago, and the detectives knew they had yet another new murder case to add to the Gecht gang's appalling list. They got a few details, enough to determine that it was an Area Six case. A quick call to Area Six gave them the name. Rose Beck Davis, a thirty-year-old advertising executive. Her mangled body had been found on September 8, exactly two months earlier. Area Six detectives promised to gather their files on the Davis case, and come over to Area Five first thing in the morning.

Finally, Detective Flynn broke off the questioning and allowed Andy to take a nap. The detectives were being very careful that all three of their prisoners were well-fed and rested. They weren't taking any chances of losing a conviction down the line because of the treatment the suspects were receiving.

Meanwhile, at Area Six, detectives were pulling out their files on the still unsolved murder of Rose Beck Davis.

Chapter Twenty-three

September 7, 1982

Rose Davis called her husband, Darrell, and told him not to expect her until late. She was driving from their Broadview home into the Chicago Loop to meet with a hotel client and would probably stay in the city through dinner and drinks.

Darrell Davis smiled to himself and asked her about her business meeting, but he didn't warn her to watch out for herself; he didn't have to. Mrs. Rosemarie Beck Davis was a free spirit, and a strong one. She said what she thought and did what she chose; she had a Bette Midler kind of quality about her that her friends and her husband loved. So, Darrell wished her success and offered his love. He would be there when she came home.

Rose drove her 1979 VW Rabbit confidently through Chicago's Loop traffic toward the Near North Raddison Hotel. Even though she and Darrell lived in the west suburban town of Broadview, Chicago's downtown traffic didn't intimidate her; it was simply one more challenge to be dealt with, and Rose Davis loved a challenge. At thirty years of age, Rose was five eight and a reed-thin 119 pounds. She wore her light brown hair cropped nearly into a crewcut. She'd had her left ear pierced for three earrings and her right ear for one, just to be different. And inside her left wrist she had tattooed the *om* symbol, a Hindu symbol for eternity.

Rose was giftedly artistic, a graduate of the Southern Illinois School of Graphic Design, and she was confident. She had successfully designed shopping center window displays, had designed her own wedding dress, a slim, stylish affair of heavy satin, and she had now become involved in a business that wholesaled theater and sports-events tickets to high-class hotels. This was an important meeting coming up this evening, and she was eager to get it started.

Rose parked her VW at 71 East Goethe, a posh, narrow, exclusive lane of luxurious apartment buildings just off Chicago's spectacular Lake Shore Drive. The Raddison Hotel was just down the street.

She and Angie Colucci, the hotel's sales manager, hit it off right away, and their business was soon concluded. They decided to see a little of the famous Rush Street nightclub area and then go for dinner. As they strolled from one fashionable nightclub to the next, Angie suddenly recognized a man she'd gone to high school with, and he was happy to join them in their walk. The threesome decided to have dinner at the Avenue One Restaurant in the Drake Hotel, but were refused admittance to the exclusive eatery because Angie's classmate was not wearing a tie.

Not one to be daunted by trivial details, Rose simply marched out into the hotel lobby and approached the first man coming in the door.

"Hello, are you staying here in the hotel?" she asked him brightly. When he smiled and said that he was, Rose offered to buy him dinner if he would lend their companion a tie. The man laughingly agreed, and the deal was done.

His name was *Martin Davidson, and he was a businessman from Switzerland who'd come to Chicago for the annual Housewares Show at McCormick Place. The huge Lakefront exhibition center, with nearly a half-million square feet of show space, attracted conventions from all over the world, and the Housewares Show was one of the biggest.

The foursome had a lavish meal at Avenue

One, though Davidson felt somewhat uncomfortable because of his poor command of
English. He spoke fluent German, French,
and Italian, and his English was passable
but formal. He missed many of the witti-
cisms being bandied around by his dinner
companions, and several times he felt self-
conscious, sure that they were laughing at
him. But he was alone in a strange country,
and he was grateful for the company.

After dinner, Rose and Angie suggested
they walk down to the beachfront and stroll
along Lake Michigan. Both women took their
shoes off, and the four dinner companions
walked on the sand and looked up at the
awesome display of lighted skyscrapers that
rimmed Chicago's lakefront like a jeweled
necklace. Finally, at two-thirty, they decided
to call it a night. As they walked back, Rose
and Martin Davidson fell behind their companions, as Rose kept stopping to look at the
window displays of the exclusive Michigan
Avenue shops. Angie and her friend, now
several blocks ahead, turned, but not seeing
the couple, hailed a cab.

Davidson walked Rose to within sight of
her car. He politely suggested that she might
wish to accompany him back to his hotel,
but Rose said no. She was going home to her
husband. Davidson bowed and kissed her
hand, thanking her for a lovely evening, and

then he turned and walked toward the Drake Hotel. Rose walked toward her car.

As she stood, fishing in her purse for her keys, a red van turned the corner and slowly cruised up alongside her. Two men were in the front seat. The passenger rolled down his window, and the driver leaned across him. "Hi," he said. "Want to have some fun?"

"No!" Rose said sharply as she turned away from them and reached down to put her key in the car door.

The van screeched to a stop and the passenger jumped out. Another man leaped from the rear of the van.

At eight-thirty the next morning, Area Six detective Carey Orr and his partners were having breakfast when Orr's pager went off. He called his office.

"Looks like we got a jumper," he told his partners as he came back to the table. "Twelve-fifty Lake Shore Drive. A garbageman found the body in a gangway. Do you believe it?"

People generally didn't leap to their deaths on the wealthiest street in the city.

When the detectives turned onto Goethe, they were amazed. Squad cars, reporters' cars, camera trucks and vans, clogged the narrow street for two full blocks. They had to park and walk. This was no jumper.

She lay in the gangway, in a half-sitting position against the building, her head slumped to the left. A black sock was tied around her neck, another around her left wrist. Her slacks and panties were tangled around her left foot. Her blue-and-black-striped sweater and her bra were tangled over her right arm. Blood had pooled between her legs. Her nose and her eye sockets were crushed, teeth lay loose in her broken jaws, and her face was unrecognizable. Long, deep lacerations scored her breasts, and there were a number of small puncture wounds in her abdomen. Blood spatters pocked the brick wall two feet high and nine feet around. She had no purse and, strangely, no shoes.

Darrell Davis and Rose's friends had been calling back and forth frantically since early morning, looking for her. Now they heard the broadcasts on WBBM All-News Radio about a woman's apparently murdered body having been found on Lake Shore Drive. They made the call and learned the worst. The *om* tattoo on the inside of her left wrist confirmed it; Rosemarie Beck Davis had been savagely murdered.

Coincidentally, Special Agent Robert Ressler from the FBI Behavioral Sciences Unit was in Chicago, just beginning to teach Chicago detectives about profiling, the art of

looking at a victim at a crime scene and de-
ducing therefrom a "profile" of the offender.
The detectives called and Ressler, together
with Chicago's FBI supervising special agent
Robert Sigalski, agreed to come out.

After studying Rose Davis's body and the
surrounding environment, Ressler said that
several things stood out; the viciousness of
the assault on Rose's face contrasted
sharply with the hesitant tentativeness of
the superficial wounds on her abdomen.

"You're looking for a man who's unsure
about his sexuality," Ressler told the detectives. "He's probably small, skinny, with effeminate features, bisexual most likely,
maybe a latent homosexual, but probably
not openly homosexual."

Area Six detectives immediately saturated
the neighborhood in a canvass, seeking anyone who had seen or heard anything. While
that was going on, they quickly zeroed in on
Martin Davidson, the Swiss businessman,
Rose Davis's last known companion.

Davidson was cooperative but terrified. He
was in a foreign country, uneasy with the
language, and being questioned about a terrible murder. Area Six detectives brought in
a German-speaking police officer to act as
translator while Davidson told his version of
the night's events.

While Davidson was being interviewed,

teams of Area Six detectives were continuing the neighborhood canvass, with some interesting results. The tenant in a garden apartment, a young male hairdresser employed by the prestigious Marshall Field's, said that he'd heard a "loud female scream" and then "moaning noises" about 3:00 A.M. outside his bedroom window, which faced the gangway where Rose had been found.

The hairdresser, *Jacques Monaco, went on to say that upon being awakened, he'd gone into the kitchen to make himself a cup of tea.

"A cup of tea?" the detectives asked. "You mean you heard a woman screaming right outside your window and you went into the kitchen for a cup of *tea*?"

"Well," Monaco said, "I guess I did sort of peep out the window to see what was going on."

Monaco said he'd gone into the bathroom next to his bedroom, removed shampoo and other toiletries from the windowsill, and looked out into the gangway, where, he claimed, he saw nothing. He said the "moaning noises" went on for about fifteen or twenty minutes. The detectives were disgusted, but not too surprised at Monaco's account of his actions. He certainly wasn't the first city dweller lately to witness somebody being killed and do nothing to help.

After he made his cup of tea, Monaco said, he'd called his girlfriend. She was enraged that he would call at such an hour and hung up on him. Then he sat in the kitchen and listened to the noises in the gangway.

While they were interviewing Monaco, the detectives noticed that in addition to the black leather pants he was wearing, Monaco also owned a black leather dog collar with silver spikes that was lying on the coffee table. He didn't have a dog.

Monaco suddenly changed his story again, now claiming that when he'd looked out his bathroom window, he had seen one of his coworkers, a fellow hair stylist from Field's, struggling with someone in the gangway. Pressed, he admitted that he'd been having trouble with this man at work, and maybe he hadn't seen him at all. Maybe he'd just "dreamed" the whole thing.

His equivocations made no sense, but about one point Monaco was adamant; at no time that night had he left the apartment.

Meanwhile, the investigation of the Swiss businessman Martin Davidson continued. With his permission, the detectives impounded the clothing he'd been wearing when he was with Rose Davis. His clothes were sent to the crime lab for analysis, but no trace of blood was found, which would have been a near impossibility had he been at the slaughterhouse scene of Rose Davis's death. Davidson also agreed to a polygraph exam, which he passed with no indication of knowledge of or participation in her murder. Finally, three days after Rose Davis's murder, Davidson was released and allowed to return to Switzerland. It is presumed he never forgot his trip to Chicago.

When the detectives made their first canvass of the plush Lake Shore Drive neighborhood, some of the residents weren't at home. Three days later, they came back, looking for—anything. And they found it.

A young woman who lived diagonally across the street from the gangway where Rose Davis's body had been found said that she'd been out with friends for dinner and bowling that night. While she lived in the middle of the block, her friends had dropped her off at the corner, since the street was so narrow and parking was impossible. They watched as she walked to her apartment building, then she waved them good night.

One thing she did notice, though, she now told the Area Six detectives, was that the man from the 1250 building was standing outside on the sidewalk. She particularly noticed him, she told detectives, because he had been wearing black leather pants and a black leather dog collar with silver studs. She'd seen him in the outfit before. No, she said, he wasn't doing anything, he was just sort of ambling back and forth and looking into the gangway.

After learning all this, and combined with Ressler's unofficial profile, Area Six detectives zeroed in on Jacques Monaco. He agreed to take the polygraph, which showed him being deceptive in having left his apartment during the time of the murder and in having seen anything in the gangway. The polygraph indicated, however, that Monaco was telling the truth when he said he hadn't killed Rose Beck Davis.

Difficult as it was to believe, the only explanation seemed to be that Monaco had heard the initial attack in the gangway, got up and put on his leather outfit, and gone outside to stand around and watch the murder. Such behavior defied reason, but it was the only logical explanation. A telephone call from Monaco to 911 would have surrounded the gangway where Rose Beck Davis was being murdered with dozens of squad cars in a matter of moments. That call had never been made.

Further horror was added when Dr. Robert Stein, the Cook County medical examiner, released his autopsy report. According to Dr. Stein, "the vaginal area was totally covered with blood, lacerated and hemorrhaged. A pint of blood and a piece of broken lumber measuring four inches in length were found in the lesser pelvis. The wood extended through the vagina, the uterus and a portion of the small intestine. Two pieces of wood were found up in the abdominal cavity . . . contusions on both legs, fractured skull and massive subdural hemorrhage." Rose Beck Davis had been tortured to death.

Chapter Twenty-four

It was 2:30 A.M. Andy Kokoraleis slept in Interrogation Room E. In Room F, right next door, Eddie Spreitzer was sound asleep.

Detective Tom Flynn walked the floor and drank coffee.

"God," he said to no one in particular. It seemed that no matter how vicious a criminal was, there was always someone else who had done worse. But this, he thought, was about as bad as it got.

Over to the side of the room, Warren Wilkosz sat with Cook County detective Larry Troka. The men were going over what was known so far about the murder of Shui Mak. They both looked up when they heard Flynn muttering. They knew what he was feeling—they shared it—but there was nothing to say.

"Go home," Flynn heard. It was Minogue.

"Huh?"

"Go home. You've been working for three

199

days and nights. How much sleep have you had?"

"None to speak of."

"Then go," Minogue said. "We start again in the morning."

Flynn didn't want to leave in the middle of the case that Andy Kokoraleis was building against himself, but he realized he was just too weary to think straight. He took his coat and left, promising to be back as soon as he'd had a couple hours' sleep.

For a few hours, the detective room was dimmed and quiet. A single Area Five detective kept watch and answered the occasional telephone. Wilkosz and Detective Troka talked quietly between themselves in hushed tones.

Troka was talking to Wilkosz about all that he had put into the investigation of Shui Mak's death, until it had become a personal cause that nearly obsessed him. Wilkosz knew what his fellow detective meant: he, too, had answered dozens of calls from the Mak family, calls during which they begged and pleaded with him to find their Shui. They offered to say prayers for him, they offered to pay him, they would have offered anything they had in the world, but he couldn't help them.

Troka told Wilkosz that he had spent weeks interviewing people in the large Oriental enclaves in Hanover Park and its adjoining suburbs. Largely because of the church-sponsored sanctuary movement, large pockets of Vietnamese, Koreans, Cambodians, Laotians, and Chinese now made their homes in the suburbs. They were extraordinarily courteous and law-abiding people who tended to keep to themselves and settle their problems without resorting to the police. No one knew anything about the disappearance of Shui Mak. It was as though she had vanished off the face of the earth.

Detective Troka had persuaded the Chicago Police Department to publish a special daily bulletin with Shui's picture and information on it, hoping somebody in the huge city had seen something. Sixteen thousand bulletins went out, but he never received a single call in response.

Then, on September 30, her body had been found in Barrington, one of the most exclusive suburbs in the state.

The skeleton lay in pieces, with several of the larger arm and leg bones lying some distance away. Troka surmised that small animals had been at the body. Each bone was bleached white and clean. Long black hair covered the skull, and the shreds of a red sweater clung to the upper portion of the body.

Around the neck of the skeleton was a yellow metal chain with a green heart-shaped opaque stone. Troka took the necklace as evidence, along with several strands of sharp wire that lay near the body. Dr. Robert Stein, at the Cook County Medical Examiner's Office, found, besides extensive facial injuries, a deep horseshoe-shaped crack on the back of the skull several inches in diameter that had pierced almost all the way through the thick bone.

Detective Troka took the necklace to a jeweler to be examined, and the results were puzzling. The jeweler said that the chain was twenty-four-carat gold and the stone heart was a fine-quality jade. Twenty-four-carat gold, the jeweler explained to the detective, is not manufactured or sold in the United States because it is considered too malleable, too soft for use in jewelry. But many other countries do sell jewelry of this gold. The jade, too, was of a quality rarely seen in U.S. jewelry stores.

The stone commonly known as jade, the jeweler explained, can actually be either of two stones: jadeite or nephrite, which is sometimes called ax-stone. The finest and most expensive jade is jadeite of a clear emerald or apple green color and possessed of a nearly translucent quality, with chrome pigment running through it. It comes from Burma and is known as imperial jade. The heart attached to the gold chain was imperial jade.

Given the twenty-four-carat gold chain, the imperial jade, and the victim's waist-length blue-black hair, Detective Troka called for assistance from Dr. Clyde Snow, a forensic anthropologist who frequently assisted medical examiners' offices throughout the country in the identification of human remains.

Forensic anthropology was a fairly new science, recognized by the American Academy of Sciences only in 1972 as a separate branch of anthropology.

Dr. Snow told Detective Troka that the skeleton was of an Oriental woman in her late twenties or early thirties. Troka contacted the Mak family, who gave him the name of Shui's dentist in Chicago's Chinatown. Troka went to Chinatown, and, walking among the colorful red dragon-spired restaurants and shops toward the dentist's office, he knew what the outcome was going to be, and he was right. Shui Mak had been found at last.

"The thing that's driven me crazy all these months," Troka now told Wilkosz in the dim quiet at Area Five, "was that upside-down horseshoe-shaped crack in her skull. I couldn't figure out what in the hell caused it. I ran around to tool experts and museum anthropologists and every detective who would listen to me."

"And now you know," Wilkosz said.

"Yeah, now I know." Eddie Spreitzer had said that he and Robin Gecht punched Shui so hard in the face that the back of her head "bounced off the van." Troka had gone to the evidence garage and measured, but he was already sure he had his answer. The bulging hinge on the side door of the van was just five feet off the ground. Thus, the upside-down crack that split the back of Shui's head open.

"I only hope that blow against the hinge killed her," Troka said as the two men put their coats on and walked out, waving good night to the detective at the desk.

"I know," Wilkosz said. "Let's hope she never knew what came next."

At dawn, detectives began wandering in and by eight o'clock the squad room was buzzing again. Area Five detectives John Philbin and Allen Thiel were assigned to continue processing Andy Kokoraleis's statement. Assistant State's Attorney Robert Bastone would be back later to take Andy's formal confession. This was police work, slow, arduous, repetitious, but necessary.

At eight forty-five, Philbin and Thiel woke Andy up and took him downstairs to the lockup to be fingerprinted and photographed. Andy had the standard lockup meal, a baloney sandwich on white bread.

When Philbin explained that he and his partner would be conducting the next portion of Andy's statement, Andy said he would try to be truthful.

"But the truth is me and Robin and Eddie did so many murders, the details get mixed up in my mind."

"How many, Andy?" Philbin asked.

"Seventeen, eighteen, I don't know. Maybe more."

"Andy seemed sad," Philbin says. "But at the same time I think he was relieved, relieved that finally it was all over."

When they got upstairs to Interrogation Room E, Philbin said, "Andy, I want you to pick out a particular incident that you remember clearly, and let's talk about it."

Crying now, Andy said he remembered the night on Rush Street when he, Robin, and Eddie grabbed a woman.

"Did you kill her?"

"Yes."

Philbin wanted someone from Area Six to sit in while Andy described the murder of Rose Beck Davis, and he knew just who he wanted. He took a break and called Sergeant Ed Flynn in Area Six. Sergeant Flynn (no relation to Tom Flynn) came right over. He was a slight, compact, articulate man, and when he got to Area Five, he sat with Andy Kokoraleis alone for a while in Room E.

Sergeant Flynn, with teenage boys of his own, knew how to talk to young men, and he felt he was developing an understanding of Andy as they talked. But when he came out of the room, after a half hour of harrowing details, he was as shaken as the other detectives had been.

"Andy was a wimp posing as a tough guy," Sergeant Flynn says. "But he was a boy who'd had some upbringing, some sense of family and of moral values. It was obvious he feared Robin Gecht, but he hated him, too. He hated the terrible things he'd done, and he hated that he'd done them only at Robin's bidding.

"I didn't get the feeling Andy was confessing out of a sense of philanthropy. It was more like, 'This guy Robin is so nuts and so scary, is he going to come after me next? Is he going to do to me what we did to all those women?' Andy had gotten himself into something that was way beyond him, and he seemed, not happy exactly, but kind of relieved, like finally, it was all over."

When A.S.A. Bastone arrived at Area Five, he and Sergeant Flynn sat in Room E with Andy. Bastone explained to Andy that he was not Andy's lawyer, but was here to as-

sist the police officers. Again, careful police
procedure so that there could be no criticism
down the line. Bastone read the Miranda
warnings to Andy and waited until Andy said
that he understood his rights under each
question. Then the interrogation began.

Andy said that in September, he, Robin,
and Eddie had been cruising the Rush Street
area, looking for a woman to pick up. He
then went on to describe their abduction of
Rose Beck Davis, and he gave the detectives
an explanation of the shards of wood found
in Mrs. Davis's intestinal and abdominal
cavities. Robin Gecht, Andy said, had a
home-made tool that he carried with him, a
type of ax with a wooden handle. Andy and
Eddie had held the woman down while
Robin repeatedly jammed the handle of the
ax up inside her. Then, Andy continued, he
had stabbed her in the stomach several
times "because Robin told me to."

"I felt sick then," Andy said. "I went to the
back of the van." It was five or six minutes
later that Robin and Eddie came back. Eddie
was carrying the weapons and Robin had the
woman's shoes. Eddie looked sick, too, Andy
said, but Robin was giggling.

Andy then described Linda Sutton's murder. He and Eddie had held her down, he
said, but Robin had killed her, punching her
in the face and hitting her with his home-

made ax. It was Robin, he said, who had cut off her breasts.

At this point Bastone asked Andy about the bodies in Schiller Woods.

"Can you find them for us, Andy?"

Andy said he thought he might be able to point out the various burial sites if he saw them again.

At four-thirty, Philbin, Thiel, A.S.A.'s Bastone and Beuke, and Andy Kokoraleis drove to Schiller Woods. Detectives Flynn and Murphy and Sergeant Ed Flynn followed them.

At Schiller Woods, Andy directed the men to an area about twenty-five yards into the forested area that he said looked familiar. He thought it looked like where they had buried a black hooker. The detectives dug for a half hour but found nothing. They were not surprised. The forest preserve had literally hundreds of small clearings, and it was impossible to tell one from another.

When they got back to Area Five at six-thirty, the downstairs desk personnel called up to say that Andy's father was there and wanted to see him. Detective Philbin went downstairs and escorted Mr. Kokoraleis up to the detective squad room and into Interrogation Room E.

When Mr. Kokoraleis came out fifteen minutes later, he was crying and trembling so badly that several detectives had to support him or he would have fallen.

There was a hush in the room. Nearly all the men had kids of their own, and they couldn't imagine what it must feel like to learn, after years of working and struggling to raise your children right, that your son was a monster.

Chapter Twenty-five

"It was about three weeks ago," *Edith McBride said to Detective Warren Wilkosz. They were in the living room of her Villa Park apartment. She was twenty-eight, a housewife, and she was one of dozens of people Wilkosz and Sam had talked to about Robin Gecht.

"I left my house real early," she said. "About five in the morning. I had to get some milk, and I wanted to get to the store and back before the kids got up for breakfast."

Wilkosz and John Sam were canvassing the western suburbs while the Area Five detectives interrogated Andy Kokoraleis. He and Sam were compiling background information on the murder crew. They knew that after Chicago charged Gecht's crew with the Cook County murders, DuPage would be moving in with charges in the Lorry Ann Borowski and Linda Sutton cases.

"I was walking toward my car," McBride

211

said. "I keep it in the rear parking lot. Robin Gecht pulled up next to me. He's got that red van, you know? Well, he said hello, and I said hello. Then he opened the driver's door of his van. I couldn't believe it. There was blood all over his jacket and on his jeans. And his hands were dripping with blood and it was on the window and the door. I thought at first he was hurt, but then I could see that he wasn't. It was somebody else's blood! My heart was just pounding. Robin asked me to sit in the van with him, you know, just to talk to him. I turned and ran! I jumped in my car and got out of the parking lot as fast as I could."

Good idea, Wilkosz thought. If McBride had gotten into Robin's van, she probably wouldn't be sitting here today talking about it. It troubled Wilkosz for a moment that McBride hadn't called the police to report what she'd seen, but he didn't want to waste more than a passing thought about it. During his career he had asked that simple question of people a hundred times: "Why didn't you just call the police?" The answers varied from an embarrassed shrug to a lengthy and convoluted justification, but the underlying cause was always the same. How many people have been robbed, raped, maimed, or killed because somebody else "just didn't want to get involved"? It is a question without an answer, and it has always baffled police officers.

But what was really troubling Wilkosz was the timing McBride was describing. None of the known murders they were investigating had happened during the two- or three-day period of time McBride was ascribing in her dawn meeting with Robin Gecht. In fact, the timing would place it after his attack on Denise Gardner but before his arrest for that crime. Wilkosz, like all the detectives on the case, had been hoping that Andy's "seventeen or eighteen murders" was an exaggeration, that it was some kind of sick boasting. But more and more, Wilkosz and the others were coming to the same conclusion: Robin Gecht and his crew had killed many more women than those the authorities knew about. How many? Where and when? He was coming to the conclusion that, probably, no one would ever know.

Later that afternoon, Wilkosz got a call from Area Five detective Mike Herigodt.

"Robin Gecht has a new line," Herigodt said.

"Oh, great. What is it now?"

"He says we shouldn't be looking at him for these murders. Says maybe we ought to be looking at *Thomas McCaffrey."

"Is that a fact? Who the hell is Thomas McCaffrey?" Wilkosz asked.

"Gecht's brother-in-law. He's got a live-in lover name of George. Couple of our guys are on their way out to pick them up."

Wilkosz drove into Chicago and waited at Area Five for the interrogation of Thomas McCaffrey.

McCaffrey, Rosemary Gecht's brother, was chalk white, black-haired, and thin, almost to the point of emaciation. He appeared extremely effeminate, with fluttering hands and delicate, coquettish looks. And when the police picked him up, he was furious that Robin would try to implicate him and his lover, George, in such horrible crimes. In return, he had his own stories to tell about his brother-in-law.

McCaffrey told Wilkosz and the others that he and George had been living in the basement of Robin's McVicker Street home since January 1982.

"Robin is strange," he told detectives. "I mean, very, very strange. I remember on September 19—I remember the date because it's my birthday—Robin and Eddie pulled up in the van about four-thirty in the morning. They were absolutely filthy, covered with mud. I heard Robin come downstairs to use the washing machine."

"So?"

"Well, I thought that was a little strange, don't you? Robin never washed clothes, ever, let alone at four-thirty in the morning. Robin is one sick puppy, I'm telling you. Rosemary showed me wounds in her breasts, cuts that were becoming infected, for God's sake. Robin done them. She told me. That was practically the only way he wanted sex. Sometimes I could hear her screaming at night."

McCaffrey told the detectives that he believed Eddie Spreitzer was Robin's lover, and that Andy Kokoraleis had been Robin's previous lover. He said Andy had written a love letter to Robin. McCaffrey talked for a while, relating incident after bizarre incident in the domestic affairs of the Gecht household. When his statement was over, McCaffrey voluntarily submitted to a lie-detector test, which he easily passed.

Wilkosz's instincts told him that McCaffrey was clean. Once more he was reminded that Robin Gecht was a calculating demon, trying this time to implicate his wife's brother, hoping probably that the police would zero in on McCaffrey simply because he was homosexual. That was not to be the case.

But what was becoming clearer to the detectives as they were able to put McCaffrey's revelations together with everything else they knew was some insight into the sexual disorientation of Gecht himself. He was obviously bisexual, but it was not this fact that drove him to sadistic and murderous extremes. More to the point, much of his destructiveness came from his ambivalence about exactly *what* he was. This, psychologists say, seems to be the case with many sexual psychopaths and other tormented spirits. Often it is not what a person is that makes him sociopathically ill, it is his inability to accept, to come to terms, with it. Human sexuality is a primitive, powerful drive, and when one's mind despises what one's own body desires, havoc can be the result.

Wilkosz went back to his canvass of the Anzak buildings. There he and Sam found a woman who said she had been Robin's girlfriend from July through December 1981. She said that during that time they'd had intercourse only twice. "He didn't seem to be interested in it," she said. "Mostly he talked about his guns, and about drugs. He claimed he could get any drug he wanted from a pharmacist friend of his."

Wilkosz talked with a friend of Elizabeth Kokoraleis, who was Andy's sister and Eddie's girlfriend. Elizabeth's friend said that Eddie had shown up for Elizabeth's prom with blood all over his mouth, shocking all the other students. He seemed pleased at the reaction he got, and refused to wash the blood off all evening, bragging that he'd been involved in satanic animal slaughters out in the woods. The other kids believed him without hesitation. Eddie had been considered a "major geek" by his fellow students all his school life.

Each person Wilkosz interviewed supplied the names of other people who would have information. As he and Sam went from one to the next, the stories grew more and more bizarre. There were ceremonies, they were told. There were orgies involving Gecht's sister-in-law and her circle of friends.

Finally Wilkosz talked with the guidance counselor at Willowbrook High School.

The counselor told him that a satanic fad had been sweeping through the school in recent years. Students were wearing pentagrams, carving 666 into desks, drawing inverted crosses on their hands with ballpoint pens. She had heard some of the teenagers whispering arcane oaths at one another when they passed in the halls. There was constant talk of ceremonies, witchcraft, and candles, talk that would suddenly stop when a teacher approached. In the large, forested area behind the high school, teachers had found smoldering campfires, circles of stones, odd bits of cloth nailed to trees, and sometimes the skeletons of dogs and cats.

"Satanic rituals," she explained. "It's very, very disturbing. Teenagers have a secret life, and that is okay to a certain extent, but this trend is extremely unhealthy."

Unhealthy, Wilkosz thought. There's an understatement.

Wilkosz then interviewed Patricia McCaffrey, Rosemary's mother. Mrs. McCaffrey said that Robin suffered from frequent and serious headaches. She said that Robin had met her daughter Rosemary through her neighbor, *Mrs. Hooks, when Rosemary was sixteen years old. Rosemary ran away from home with Robin. Mrs. McCaffrey said that when Robin was a teenager, his father had thrown him out of the house, and Robin had gone to live with a man named *Thomas Farley, whom the Gecht family had known when they used to live in the same apartment building. She also said that Robin had disappeared for several weeks in April 1982. When he returned, he refused to explain this sudden and extended disappearance, saying only that he'd been doing electrical work in Wisconsin.

Wilkosz was in constant contact with Area Five, and when he passed on this latest bit of information they immediately picked up Thomas Farley for questioning.

Farley, a fifty-five-year-old open homosexual, said he'd met the Gecht family when

they lived in a two-bedroom apartment at El-
ston and Diversey. Robin was the oldest of
seven kids, all of whom seemed to be constantly hungry and in need of new shoes.
The kids were in and out of his place all the
time. When Robin was seventeen, his father,
Jacob, threw him out of the house, and
Robin came to live with Farley. There'd been
some trouble with a bad check, and Farley
said he'd made it good.

Farley said that when Robin was eighteen,
he had fathered a boy with a southern girl
named Judy. Shortly after the boy, Rubin,
was born, Judy left Robin and moved back
down South.

According to Thomas Farley, there was a
definite change in Robin after he moved to
Villa Park. Suddenly, it seemed, all he talked
about was pills. He was always high, and he
had endless streams of teenage boys and
girls staying at his house. He was very crude
around teenage girls, always talking about
how much he liked "big boobs."

Farley also told the detectives that Robin
liked to brag about the women he had ripped
off. He talked about a woman named Ruth
who had hired him to do some home-repair
work. Ruth had three daughters, and Robin
bragged that he'd gotten her to buy him two
cars, pay to have his teeth fixed, and then
he stiffed her for $6,000.

Robin had also bragged about a woman he'd met in 1979. He convinced her that he was going to divorce Rosemary and marry her daughter. This woman bought him a blue van from Long Chevrolet in Elmhurst. Robin skipped out with the van and never heard from her again. Then he bragged about a woman in Berwyn who gave him $1,500 up front for remodeling work. He never did the work and she never filed a complaint. It was difficult to say which aspect gave Gecht more pleasure—being able to rip off women or knowing that they took it in silence. His latest conquest was Bridget Ross, who'd mortgaged her home to pay off his $5,000 bond for the Denise Gardner attack.

Farley said that Robin had obtained a contract for remodeling work with several Denny's restaurants, and that he constantly talked about how easy it was to meet women this way. It was at Denny's that Robin had met Tina, a young waitress who would soon bear his child.

Asked about guns, Farley said he'd seen two rifles in Robin's house on McVicker. He'd also seen Robin with a BB pistol. Farley himself had gotten rid of two BB pistols he'd found when Robin was living with him. He also said that several months previously, Eddie Spreitzer had told him that Robin bought handcuffs by the boxful and kept them in his home.

The detectives asked Farley about Robin's wife. He said he'd known Rosemary since she was sixteen years old. Rosemary was continually threatening to leave Robin because of his constant involvement with other women. But Farley felt that Rosemary got her kicks from tracking down Robin's numerous girlfriends and making friends with them.

Farley said that Rosemary had told him some time before that she'd spilled hot coffee on her breast and that the wound had become infected. Farley had driven her to West Suburban Hospital for treatment. Later, Rosemary said she'd contracted gonorrhea from Robin, and Farley took her to Northwest Hospital, where she was admitted for treatment.

When Robin had been arrested on October 20 for the attack on Denise Gardner, Rosemary, enraged, told Farley that she was going to go to the police and tell them that the wounds in her breasts were actually caused by cuts inflicted by Robin. Apparently, she had changed her mind.

Farley told the detectives he'd previously talked with Rosemary several months before when she'd called him and asked that their telephone be cut off. Farley had been paying the Gechts' phone bills because they couldn't get credit in their own name.

Rosemary said she'd been getting calls from two girls, one eighteen years old and the other nineteen. Both girls said they thought they were pregnant by Robin. Farley had the phone cut off. Two days later, Rosemary called again to say she wasn't mad at Robin anymore and she wanted her telephone back on. Farley refused, and Rosemary became angry and wouldn't speak to him again—until Robin's arrest for Denise Gardner, when Rosemary called and asked for $5,000 for bond money. Farley refused, Rosemary hung up on him, and that had been his last contact with the Gecht household.

While Chicago detectives were interviewing Thomas Farley, Detective Wilkosz was continuing his investigation in the western suburbs. Everywhere he went, the name *Billy Montgomery kept coming up. Montgomery, who was living in the Anzak buildings, had been with Robin constantly, he'd worked for Robin.

Wilkosz picked Montgomery up for questioning. At first Billy seemed cooperative. He'd known Robin Gecht since the fall of 1980, when Robin had been doing construction work on the Anzak buildings. Montgomery said he knew Andy and Eddie through

Robin. He also knew Tina, Robin's girlfriend, and Catherine, Robin's sister, who lived in the 929 building.

Billy Montgomery told Wilkosz that Robin had a way with young girls, that "he could get them to do whatever he wanted." He also talked about Eddie Spreitzer's appearance at the prom with blood all over his face.

It was when Detective Wilkosz mentioned the murders that Billy Montgomery became very upset. Wilkosz asked Montgomery if he would be willing to submit to a polygraph, and Montgomery agreed. At Fred Hunter and Associates Polygraph Examiners, Montgomery was questioned about the murders. In the opinion of Fred Hunter, Montgomery failed the polygraph as to being present and participating in the murders. Montgomery continued to deny any involvement, and when Wilkosz took him back to the DuPage Sheriff's Office, a large contingent of Montgomery's family and friends was there. They started a fight in the lobby, and all the detective personnel, deputies, and lockup personnel poured out into the lobby to contain them. Since the detectives really had nothing on him except the polygraph, not admissible evidence, Billy Montgomery was released, pending further investigation.

In continuing his canvass, Wilkosz came across a young woman who said that in the fall of 1981, she and a group of friends were at a relative's farm in Hampshire, Illinois. Eddie Spreitzer was part of the group. After a while the girls started teasing Eddie, calling him a sissy. Eddie became infuriated.

"I am not a sissy," he shouted. "I've killed somebody already!"

The girls continued to giggle. Eddie was the nerdiest guy they knew. They taunted him: "Sure, Eddie! We don't believe you, Eddie!"

"I did," he insisted. "I've killed a couple of broads. I cut their breasts off."

The girls laughed. "The whole thing, Eddie, or just the nipple?" They were skipping around him now, teasing.

"Why would you do something like that?" one girl laughed. "It's so messy!"

Suddenly, Eddie became quiet, hollow. "I don't know," he said. "The blood was just squirting out. I don't know why I did it, I just did."

Chapter Twenty-six

Robin Gecht, the man who committed some of the most monstrous crimes of our time, was born at Illinois Masonic Hospital in northwest Chicago on November 30, 1953. Though his childhood was dotted with small and large tragedies, there is nothing that makes his villainy even remotely understandable. Perhaps in his case, as in so many others, moral and sexual aberration resulted from a "cluster effect" of emotional and physical defects: bad genes, bad experiences, bad self-image, bad outlook, and bad luck. Each, only an individual strand, yet together they wrap like a spider's webbing, cocooning the human soul and deforming it into something never intended by nature.

After Robin's birth, his parents, Jacob and Ruth (who never married) brought their baby home to live with Jacob's parents, Rubin and Sara Gecht. From babyhood on, it was Robin's grandparents who watched after the child, while Jacob worked at a drugstore and Ruth worked as a waitress. When Robin was three years old, his brother, Everett, was born, and two years later, Ruth delivered a girl, Rachelle.

Robin recalls that his life was happy until Rachelle came along. He adored his grandparents. He loved trotting around after Grandpa Rubin, helping him water the lawn and fix things around the house. And his Grandma Sara, Robin recalls, was a sympathetic listener who always had time for the little boy. "You are my first grandchild," she would tell him. "That makes you special."

But with the arrival of Rachelle, Robin's comfortable world began to crumble. The little house was suddenly too small, and Robin found himself sleeping on a floor. His parents worked long hours, and his grandparents, it seemed, were always too busy with Rachelle and little Everett to give Robin attention. He felt lonely. He turned inward.

When Robin was six years old, tragedy struck. He was walking to the store with his mother, along with Everett and Rachelle. As his mother went into the store, carrying baby Rachelle, she told Robin, "You wait out front and keep an eye on Everett."

But Robin did not watch his brother. Instead, spotting toys in a store window, he walked off, leaving his brother behind.

Three-year-old Everett ran out into the street and was struck by a car.

Everett lived, but he suffered serious brain damage as a result of the accident. In time it became impossible for Robin's parents to take care of Everett, and the boy was sent off to an institution. Robin's mother assured Robin that the accident was not his fault, but Robin felt otherwise. He knew that if he hadn't gone down the block to look at the toys, his brother would still be home, happy and playful.

By January 1961, when another girl, Julia, was born, the extended family had moved to a slightly larger house on the northwest side of Chicago, but, with three bedrooms, it still was tight quarters for seven people. After the birth of Julia, Robin remembers not being allowed to go out after school, because he was always needed to help with his younger sisters.

In school Robin had trouble right from the beginning. He was small and skinny, and always dressed shabbily because the family was poor, so he was an easy target for bigger boys, who often tormented him. Frequently he was taunted for being Jewish. Though Jacob Gecht did not practice his religion or observe Jewish holidays, he also would not allow his family to observe Christian holidays. So Robin would be teased unmercifully

when the other kids talked about their
Christmas presents, and he had to admit
that his family had no Christmas.

In January 1964, Ruth gave birth to her
fifth child, another girl, Joann. That same
month Robin's beloved Grandma Sara, diag-
nosed with stomach cancer, was hospital-
ized. Then Robin's father also got sick. With
both Grandma Sara and Jacob in the hospital, the household was in chaos, and Robin
was denied whatever childhood was left to
him. His mother went back to waitressing to
help with the medical bills. The only shift
she could get was evenings. So Robin, at age
eleven, had to care for his younger siblings,
including a brand-new baby. He missed
many weeks of school, and when he was
sent to school, he cut more classes than he
attended.

In March, Grandma Sara died in the hospital. Robin was devastated. She had been a
gentle woman and the glue of the family.
Jacob, suffering from a blood ailment, came
home in April after four months in the hospital, but he was unable to work, and seemed
irreparably shaken by the loss of his mother.
Grandpa Rubin, too, mourned Sara's loss,
and he soon moved into a small apartment
of his own.

By now Robin was constantly in serious
trouble with school authorities. He had been

put into a remedial reading class. He was always getting into fights, which he usually lost because of his puny size. He began to steal. He set fires. And every time he got into trouble at school, he got another beating at home from Jacob.

When the school authorities could no longer control Robin, he was sent to Montefiore, a school for troubled juveniles. At Montefiore the rules were rigid and the kids were tough. Robin was always being picked on and beaten. He fared worse at Montefiore than he had in public school. Finally, he refused to attend school altogether, and he and his parents were summoned into juvenile court.

After listening to the details of the case, the juvenile court judge remanded Robin to the Parental School, a live-in facility for intransigent youths. Robin said good-bye to his mother one afternoon and did not see her for another eight months.

When his mother finally came to get him, she brought more tragic news. Grandpa Rubin had died. And only three weeks later, Robin's Aunt Alice, distraught over the deaths of both her parents in less than a year, killed herself.

Robin got in more trouble. He was taken back into juvenile court. This time the judge warned him to straighten out or he'd be back in the Parental School.

It was at this time that Robin found what he was good at. He began to putter with his grandfather's tools. He found he had a natural gift for fixing things. He was talented and he took pride in his work. He set up a worktable in a basement storeroom and began fixing things around the house. By the time Robin Gecht was fifteen, he could repair televisions and he had done all the electrical rewiring in the family basement. He still had no friends, but he had an absorbing hobby that was quickly turning into a job. Word began to get around that Robin could fix nearly anything, and he was kept busy.

When he was sixteen, Robin became a freshman at Carl Schurz High School. He still hated school and he did poorly at it. But in Shop, and Crafts and Electrical Repair, he was a whiz.

Soon Robin began a friendship with a girl who had a jealous boyfriend, and inevitably the boys got into a fight. Robin was suspended for ten days. Afraid that he would be sent back to Parental if he returned home with the news, he stayed in the apartment of Thomas Farley, a man who had lived in the same building as the Gecht family some years back. Robin had kept in touch with him. Several months after the suspension, when Robin's parents bought a house on North Spaulding, Robin did not move with them. Instead, he moved in with Farley.

When he was eighteen, Robin met a nice girl from the neighborhood, *Judy Carson, and within a year he and Judy had a child together, a little boy. But neither of the new parents was working full-time. Robin was doing odd electrical jobs here and there as he could get them, and studying for his G.E.D. at the same time. But the relationship with Judy was doomed, and finally she told Robin she'd met someone new. Within six months of their breaking up, Robin received an invitation to her wedding. He did not go.

If his romantic life was rocky, so was his work life. While working at one of his side jobs, Robin was caught by a city inspector who cited him for doing electrical work without a license. In court Robin was fined $200 and ordered not to do any more electrical work in Chicago until he had the proper training and a license. Soon he was working full-time at an auto-repair shop and doing electrical work on the side.

For the next few years Robin lived with Thomas Farley and knocked around at odd jobs. When he and Farley had a falling-out, Robin suddenly had to find a place to live. He knew his mother would let him stay awhile, but he wasn't sure that his father would be so anxious to have him around. At one point he did go home, but within hours he and his father were brawling. His father punched him in the face and threw him out of the house.

Despite his small stature, his delicate appearance, and his lack of money, Robin Gecht had always been able to attract women. His girlfriend at the time, *Sarah Gibson, was infatuated enough with him to invite Robin to move in with her and her mother, who was divorced. The mother liked Robin, and trusted him enough to co-sign for a car loan for him. Things went smoothly until Sarah began to resent the attention that Robin lavished on other women. There was a series of jealous fights, each noisier than the last, until finally Robin moved out. Again, he was without a place to stay.

Next, he moved in with his Uncle Rodger, who was his mother's younger brother. Rodger and his wife lived near the Gecht home, so Robin was able to stop by to visit his mother and sisters. He always made a point of coming by only when his father was at work.

By this time it seemed that the turbulence in Robin's life had calmed. He got along well with his uncle, and they did some home-repair work together. He worked full-time,

and was able to save money for his dream:
to open his own electrical-repair business.
Robin made up with Thomas Farley and the
two of them took a trip to Florida, where they
stayed with a friend of Farley's.

It was in early 1975, when Robin was visiting a friend, that he met Rosemary McCaffrey. Rosemary, just turned seventeen, was
estranged from her family as well, and living
with friends. She and Robin hit it off immediately. Soon they were lovers, and it was
not long before Rosemary announced that
she was pregnant. They both seemed happy
about it, and on August 23, 1975, they were
married in a City Hall ceremony. Robin and
Rosemary stayed with Robin's uncle for a
while, then finally struck out on their own.
On January 31, 1976, their first child, a
daughter, was born.

Robin's marriage to Rosemary was as
rocky as his previous relationships with
women, and for the same reason: he had a
roving eye. It seemed to Rosemary that there
was a constant stream of teenage girls flow-
ing through the house. The girls called at all
hours. They stayed at the house when they
fought with their parents. Sometimes it felt
as if Robin was running a shelter for runaway girls. At one point he was accused of
raping a fifteen-year-old at gunpoint in his

daughter's bed, but the girl later dropped the charges.

Though Rosemary threatened divorce time after time, the couple stayed together for the most part. They had two more children, another daughter and a son. At the time of Robin's October 20, 1982, arrest for the attack on Denise Gardner, Rosemary had a petition for divorce on file. After the arrest she withdrew the petition. When Robin was arrested again, on November 5, 1982, for the Cynthia Smith attack, Rosemary was forced to go back to work, first as a waitress, then a bartender, and later as the manager of a gas station. She continued to live in Chicago and she kept Robin's last name, both for herself and for her children.

Does all of this inevitably add up to a sadistic serial killer? Perhaps terrible things went on behind the closed doors of Robin Gecht's childhood. Perhaps there were moments too hideous to be remembered by Robin or the other people involved. But perhaps not. Relatively little is known about the creation of a conscience. Sociopaths, people who are seemingly born without a conscience, seem to be drawn mostly from the pool of adopted, abused, or neglected children. But relatively few of these do, in fact, become sociopaths. And, more frightening, a good many kind and wholesome families also have produced monsters. In any case, the publicly known facts about Robin Gecht's life reveal little that is not commonplace. The bizarre and barbaric way he treated his victims will, probably forever, be the subject of speculation.

"It is common for serial killers to remove body parts and use them to replay the murder scenes, sometimes to masturbate with," says Dr. Jack Levin of Northeastern University. Levin, co-author, with Jack McDevitt, of *Hate Crimes: The Rising Tide of Bigotry and Bloodshed*, is one of the nation's leading experts on serial killers.

Levin says, "In the Gainesville, Florida, murders, for example, the nipples were cut off of many of the victims. They were excised very meticulously, very surgically. To the serial killer, these body parts are souvenirs with which to reminisce about the crime. It is like a fan buying a program at a Red Sox game. Sometimes the killers take jewelry or other property."

Though we loosely refer to serial killers as psychopaths, Levin says psychopathic serial killers are rare. "The typical serial killer is a functioning person who happens to be a sociopath," he says. "He goes to church, he shows up at work, he has a social life, he is often charming and pleasant to be with. A true psychopath would probably not have the intellectual wherewithal to be a serial killer. He would be too disoriented, so confused that he would be easily spotted, and easily apprehended."

Levin says that sadism gives murderers like Gecht a feeling of being powerful and superior. He says, "Most of these guys feel a profound sense of powerlessness in their lives, which they attempt to overcome by denigrating their victims. It becomes very important that they make the victim suffer. Dominant sex and mutilation become a vehicle for having power in the world. And the more disgusting and hideous the mutilation, the more power the sadist feels. Ed Gein, for example, would take breasts and vaginas. He would even go to graves and rob body parts from corpses. Then he would dance in the moonlight in the presence of these body parts to recreate his mother, who had died."

Levin says he is not surprised that Gecht was able to recruit so many helpers for the murders.

"These people are often charismatic," he says. "Manson, for example, was able to mesmerize many people whom we would otherwise consider quite normal, including one follower who had been voted most likely to succeed, and another who had a master's degree in social work. He was able to make them feel special, important, and that's what

Gecht did. In such groups people are often able to carry out atrocities that they would never even consider on their own. It is a mob mentality that allows each individual participant to excuse his own culpability."

In fact, says Dr. Levin, Robin's crew was not at all unusual. "Most people don't realize this, but about a third of serial killers work in teams," he says. "And often the members of the team would never kill alone. The Hillside Stranglers are a case in point. These two cousins were killing women, but as far as we can tell, one of them never killed anybody after the team broke up. Often a team of serial killers has one dominant member, usually a real sadist. For some reason he has a lot of credibility, and the other members are easily persuaded to go along with his suggestions. Once they get through the first killing, it gets easier and they begin to develop their own culture, the culture of murder. And while they are together they find it quite easy to kill, in the same way a pack of wild dogs will attack prey that no single member of the pack would dare attempt alone."

Another factor that enters into the group psychology of the Robin Gecht crew is the so-called "small-man syndrome." Eddie Spreitzer, at five nine, was the tallest member of the group. Both he and Andy Kokoraleis, who was even shorter and scrawnier, had always been considered social and sexual laughingstocks by girls their own age. Robin Gecht, at five seven and just 125 pounds, had been slapped around and bullied by other boys all his school life.

FBI Supervisory Special Agent Robert Sigalski, one of the pioneers of the FBI's profiling and ViCAP programs, says: "The little man has a perception that because of his diminutive stature, he isn't going to be viewed as tough or strong, so he has to constantly put on an act, to himself and to everybody around him, about just how tough he really is. It's all about power and control."

Sigalski, at six one and weighing "more than I should," is the son of a Chicago police officer. Both Sigalski's father and grandfather were also big men, and he says: "My father and my grandfather both used to tell me all the time: 'Tough guys don't have to act tough.' You can tell a lot about a guy just by the kind of car he drives, for instance. When you see one of those cars that're all jacked up in the front and full of tassels and decorations, and they're making all kinds of noise and forcing you to notice them, you can bet that the guy who steps out of that car is going to look and act just like that—he's somebody who's trying to look and sound bigger and more important than he actually is. You rarely see a really big, really tough guy driving a car like that."

Robin Gecht, of course, drove a large, roomy van, which was perfectly normal in itself. But he, too, had "customized" his vehicle until it was no longer just a vehicle. It was his own personally designed and outfitted traveling death chamber.

Chapter Twenty-seven

"How come you wouldn't come to the police station?" Detective Cindy Pontoraro said.

She was sitting in a rear booth at the Grand-Austin Grill, a steamy all-night diner on Chicago's northwest side, with Tina, one of Robin Gecht's ex-girlfriends. Tina, sobbing hysterically, had called Area Five to say she knew some things about Robin Gecht.

"Robin would find out," Tina said.

"How?"

"He just would. He has mysterious ways." Tina kept looking back over her shoulder as she spoke.

"I see," Pontoraro said. A veteran sex-crimes detective, she was Area Five's specialist in such interviews. She didn't want to spook the girl. "Just as well," she said soothingly. "Here we can eat while we talk."

The Grand-Austin Grill, or GAG as the district police called it, features huge breakfast platters of fried potatoes and onions, spicy, greasy sausage patties, mounds of grits and butter, and down-home baking powder biscuits. The jukebox whined out Willie Nelson, Dolly Parton, and Johnny Cash.

Pontoraro could see that Tina was scared. So scared she had refused to be alone when she talked with a detective. A girlfriend of Tina's sat in a nearby booth holding Tina's baby. Pontoraro ordered coffee for herself, Tina, and Tina's friend.

"Tell me about Robin," she said. She had a soft, measured way of speaking that calmed her subjects. She also had an unthreatening look about her, direct brown eyes, short dark hair. Women knew instinctively that they could tell Detective Cindy Pontoraro just about anything; she would understand, and she would not judge.

"Robin thinks he's a ladies' man," Tina said.

"Is he?"

"Yeah, I guess. Even though he's married, that hardly slowed him down at all. He's got girlfriends everywhere."

Pontoraro understood. Though an educated, socially adept woman would see Robin Gecht as a greasy little twerp, she could see that a lonely, needy young woman with little self-esteem might be attracted to Gecht. He seemed to possess a combination of confidence and clumsiness that could bring out the mother in a woman.

Pontoraro recognized in Tina's fear-love of Robin Gecht the same unhealthy brand of self-imposed slavery that she so often saw in the prostitutes who sold their bodies, their souls, and their futures to support a pimp who in return abused and disrespected them. As a strong, successful woman, Pontoraro could feel anger that a woman would so debase herself, but her feelings toward these women was never contemptuous. They inspired in her, as in most female police officers, a frustrated empathy. And pity.

"All the time we were together," Tina went on, "Robin was married, of course, but I'd always catch him with other girls, too. He always told me I was his special lady and that he only stayed with his wife because of the kids. But then I'd turn my back and he'd be fooling around with somebody else."

Tina said she had left Robin once after one of their endless arguments about his women. Shortly after that he was arrested for molesting a fifteen-year-old girl.

"His wife told me she found blood on their daughter's bed," Tina said. "And later Robin admitted to me that he'd been with the girl. But he said it was my fault, and he was real mad at me."

"Your fault?"

"Yeah, my fault. And maybe he's right, in a way."

Maybe he's an asshole, Pontoraro thought to herself. But aloud she said: "What about drugs, Tina? Did you and Robin do drugs?"

"He always had a lot of pills. All kinds of pills. Anything you ever heard of, and lots more I didn't even know the name of. We would just drive to this drugstore over by the lake, and he would come out with as many pills as he wanted. He was always testing me out with the pills. Like, 'Take two of these and one of these,' you know? To see what was going to happen. One time he gave me some pills and I was knocked out for about three days. When I woke up, I just knew that something strange had happened to me."

Something strange? Pontoraro thought. Something strange! She wanted to shout at Tina and hug her protectively at the same time. This whole relationship with Robin Gecht was almost surrealistically strange. But she held her tongue.

"And then there was the Elvis thing."

"Elvis Presley?"

"Right," Tina said. "Robin is obsessed with Elvis. He collects Elvis stuff, pictures and rare records and coffee cups and everything. That's his special stuff and nobody is allowed to handle any of it but him. He acts as though he thinks he is Elvis. I asked him once if he believed in God, and you know what he said?"

"I can't even imagine."

"He said he only believes in two things: himself and Elvis Presley."

This, Pontoraro knew, was something that the other Area Five detectives had noticed. Robin had many things in common with Elvis—the adulation of his mother, the exaggeratedly courtly mannerisms, the sort of aw-shucks-ma'am, good ole boy image that Elvis refined and rode to stardom. Obviously, in view of Gecht's success with women, it was a stratagem that still worked.

"But the big thing with Robin," Tina said, "was the breasts."

"Tell me about it," said Detective Pontoraro.

"Well, he was obsessed with the way a woman's breasts worked. I mean, obsessed. For a long time that's all he would talk about. He was always after me to cut off one of my nipples, so he could see inside. He said that black whores did it all the time. He said if I wouldn't do it for him, he'd find someone who would."

Tina explained that she'd become pregnant with Gecht's child, and he insisted that he must see how the milk flowed into the breast.

"But then our baby was born and he just

stopped all the harassing about it. Just all of a sudden like that, bang, stop, right after the baby was born."

"When was that?" Pontoraro asked.

"Last year. April 3, 1981."

Tina's tale continued. Robin, she said, preferred sex in the van rather than in bed. They would start "fooling around," and then he would stop and both of them would have to get up and go outside to climb into the back of the van. Often, he liked to undress her just from the waist up.

"He liked to chase me around and stick pins in my breasts or sometimes he'd grab me and hurt me until I screamed in pain. One time I went by Robin's house and Robin's wife, Rosemary, came out. I told her she didn't look too good—she was pale and sweaty and sick looking. She took me inside and she lifted her blouse. She had six pins, like hat pins, stuck in her breast. She said Robin wouldn't let her take them out. She told me they bled a lot, and Robin would inject her with novocaine so it wouldn't hurt so bad."

Pontoraro was appalled, and a sharp feeling of sadness washed over her for this woman, and for all those other women whose lives had been used, or ended, because of one little man's dark hungers.

"Rosemary told me she was afraid Robin

was going crazy, that he was getting worse and worse all the time. She said Robin made her bring her parents' big white dog over, and that he would have sex with the dog right in the living room. She showed me a pair of Robin's undershorts that were coated with white hairs. She said that when their own dog went into labor, Robin dragged it down into the basement and beat it to death with a baseball bat. Then he cut the dog open so he could watch the puppies being born. He put the pups in jars of alcohol and kept them on the basement shelves."

After they finished their coffee, Tina took Detective Pontoraro into the ladies' room and showed her the wounds on her breasts. Most of the cuts were knife wounds and deep, round, angry-looking pinholes. One scar on her breast was more puckered. When Pontoraro asked Tina about it, she said she'd gotten it when she and Robin had been driving in the van and he'd poured lighter fluid on her and lit it. And once, she said, when Robin had her in the back of the van, he suddenly began tying her up with a rope. He looped the rope around her breasts and tightened it until, terrified, she was able to free one hand and make him stop.

"Robin likes to make his own weapons for what he does to women," Tina said. "He calls them his 'tools.' He had this short piece of broomstick he put together with a long pin in the end. He used to chase me around and stick me with it. One night while he was sleeping I hid the stick, but Robin made another one."

Tina talked about another tool, one that she called "Robin's little home-made ax." This was a foot-long piece of broomstick with a thick, triangular piece of glass embedded at one end.

In discussing this issue of Gecht's home-made "tools," the FBI's Robert Sigalski later said: "Power and control. All of these things Gecht did to so many women was about those two things—power and control. We see that in the type of serial killer we call the 'organized type.' He fixed up his van to meet his needs, he fashioned his own weapons rather than just buy something off the shelf to serve the purpose. This type of killer is the one who will torture and torment and mutilate his victims while they're still conscious, because their fear and pain is a tremendous turn-on, a tremendous power boost, if you will. And Gecht took that lust for power a step further. Not only did he take for himself the power of life and death over someone else, he invented the very devices by which he would administer that power."

Next, Tina told Detective Pontoraro about Robin's obsession with cemeteries. She said that once they had been driving around and Robin pulled over and forced her to watch a burial at Chapel Hill Gardens. After the family had left, he spent an hour or more talking with the groundskeeper about the specifics of burials.

"He told me a story about a woman who had her husband, what do you call it, dug up . . ."

"Exhumed?"

"Yeah, that's it, exhumed. This woman had her husband exhumed once a year on his birthday so she could visit with him. Robin thought that was a really nice thing for her to do. And he told me that a good way for somebody to get rid of bodies would be to take the body to a cemetery where they already dug the grave. You know, like the night before the funeral? Then you could just put the body in the grave and throw some dirt on it and the next day the funeral would come along and put a casket right on top of it. Nobody would ever find the body you put there."

"Jesus, Tina," Pontoraro finally had to ask. "Why did you stay with him?"

Tina looked at her, frustrated, as if the answer was so obvious Pontoraro must not have been paying attention.

"You don't understand," she said, and she started to cry again. "You just don't understand. Robin has—has, I don't know what to call it, he has a power."

Pontoraro reached over and patted the distraught woman's hand.

"It's okay, Tina. Tell me about this power. How did it work?"

"Well, for one thing, he's got the power to find me anywhere I go. I left him once. Actually, I left him lots of times. But he always found me no matter where I went or what I did to get away. The last time I did it and he came and found me, he said he'd kill me if I ever tried to leave him again. He would have, too."

"How would he do that? How would the power work?"

"He always took little things from my apartment. He took a gold chain once, and a notebook, sometimes a photograph. If I would ask him about it, he'd just laugh real mean and spooky. He was using those things to control me. My family says he is evil. They won't even come near me because of Robin. They say they won't have nothing more to do with me if I'm with him."

By the time Tina finished her tale, both women were drained. Pontoraro, though she had helped her fellow detectives move a step closer to prosecuting a madman, was depressed. There seemed no bottom to man's capacity for cruel depravity.

Tina agreed to go over her statement again with an assistant state's attorney. She asked Pontoraro at least a dozen times, "You're sure that Robin won't be let out of jail?" The detective assured her that he would not, unless he could come up with $100,000 cash, ten percent of his million-dollar bond.

Pontoraro left the diner hoping she was right. Gecht had already escaped one prosecution. On the previous Monday, he had stood before Judge Joseph Urso. Gecht, smiling, watched while an assistant state's attorney asked the judge to drop the attempted-murder charge against Gecht. The Cynthia Smith case, he said, had finally unraveled. Smith had been unable to pick Gecht out of a photo lineup. Finally, she had admitted that she'd cut herself while crawling through a broken window in escaping after a burglary. Her description of Gecht had come not from being brutalized by him, but from seeing the flyers Warren Wilkosz had posted all over the West Side of Chicago.

Robin Gecht, however, was not free. The state's attorney told the court that his office was putting together a grand jury indictment. The state would say that on June 13 Robin Gecht mutilated and tried to murder Angel York. After listening to the horrid details of that attack, the judge set his bond at one million dollars.

On that same Monday morning, Police Superintendent Richard J. Brzeczek held a formal press conference in the fifth-floor auditorium at Police Headquarters. Throughout the weekend rumors had been swirling, and now the room was filled with reporters. Were these incredible tales true? they wanted to know.

Brzeczek told the press what the police knew so far. Now that the families of victims had been notified and charges had been prepared, Brzeczek was able to talk to the reporters about which mutilation murders Eddie Spreitzer and Andy Kokoraleis had confessed to.

The murders, he said, were "gruesome" and "grisly," finding that nothing he said could quite communicate the horror of what had happened. And then came the shocker. "The Chicago Police Department," he said, "is still investigating one of the suspect's claims that they had committed seventeen, eighteen, or more such murders."

Here was a story that was almost too sensational, and in the days that followed the press conference, the Chicago media struggled not with ways to play it up, but with ways to play it down. The newspapers, in particular, seemed to choke on the details.

Apparently, someone at the *Chicago Tribune* had a problem with the word *breasts,* so the paper described, instead, "the mutilation of secondary sex organs."

The case also took time to find a title. When the first articles appeared, the crimes were referred to as "Cult Murders" or "Devil Worship Cult Mutilations." Within a few days Gecht and his crew had become "Jack the Ripper–Style" slayers, then "Ripper–Style" murderers. Finally, the case came to be known in the popular press as the "Ripper Murders."

The problem with reporting on the case was not just the mutilations but also cannibalism. Eddie Spreitzer had told the police that Robin sometimes made the crew eat parts of the sliced-up breasts. How does a news outlet report all the lurid details without sounding like a supermarket tabloid? As a whole, the news organizations in Chicago took a restrained and dignified approach to the reporting.

On Tuesday, November 9, DuPage detectives Warren Wilkosz and John Sam, still deeply committed to learning more about the Ripper Murders, went to Area Five, where they formally charged Eddie Spreitzer and Andy Kokoraleis with the murders of Linda Sutton and Lorraine Ann Borowski. After that they went back to their canvassing.

They knew it would be a long time before they could pry Eddie and Andy free of Chicago, but their formal charges were in place, and when their turn came, they wanted to be ready.

Chapter Twenty-eight

On Wednesday Eddie Spreitzer and Andy Kokoraleis were indicted for murder, rape, kidnapping, and armed violence in the death of Rose Beck Davis. Eddie was also indicted for murder, rape, aggravated kidnapping, deviate sexual assault, and armed violence for Sandra Delaware's death. Though there was no shortage of murders in Chicago, these two received a lot of attention in the press. They were not just murderers; they were part of the "Ripper Murders," which by this time had been installed into the public consciousness around Chicago.

It is likely that the Ripper Murders title was invented by Phil Wattley, a longtime *Chicago Tribune* police reporter. Wattley, who for many years had worked what reporters referred to as the "cop shop" beat, took gleeful pride in assigning tag lines to particular crimes, a practice strictly forbidden by his supervisors at the *Tribune*. Wattley had come up with "Baby Moses" for a young child found abandoned along Lake Michigan, the "Gentleman Rapist" for a man who always apologized to his victims, and even the "Pork-Chop Killer" for a man who had killed his brother over who was entitled to the last pork chop.

Such appellations earned Wattley a bawling-out from time to time, and finally, he was called on the carpet by his supervisors at the *Tribune* and told he could not use a tag-line again unless the cops themselves invented it. No problem. Wattley would simply call a police officer or detective friend, who would immediately agree that he or she had invented the tag, and he was welcome to use it.

Inevitably, when word of the Ripper Murders started reverberating through the media, cranks, as well as reliable sources, began burning up the phone lines to police headquarters. Calls came in to Area Five from crackpots of every stripe who claimed to have information about Gecht and his crew. But there were also calls from rational people who had somehow brushed up against the horrors of Robin Gecht. One of those calls came from *Melanie Miller, a thirty-six-year-old nurse from Lombard.

Mrs. Miller said that her fifteen-year-old daughter, Lisa, had been best friends with

Elizabeth Kokoraleis, Andy's sister, and that Lisa had begun dating Andy some months before. In January 1982, Mrs. Miller received a telephone call from someone named Robin Gecht, whom she didn't know. Gecht asked her if Lisa could come and baby-sit for him while his wife worked.

Mrs. Miller thought it a strange request since she and Lisa lived in Lombard and Gecht lived all the way out in Chicago. She said no.

Two weeks after that, her daughter Lisa ran away with Elizabeth Kokoraleis. Mrs. Miller was frantic. When she called Elizabeth's father, Mr. Kokoraleis told her that Elizabeth was staying at Robin Gecht's house. He didn't know about Lisa. The next day Mr. Kokoraleis drove into Chicago and brought his daughter home.

Mrs. Miller still had no idea of where her own daughter was. Soon she began receiving telephone calls from Robin Gecht. He had heard about her problem, he said, and he would help her find her daughter. Mrs. Miller drove into Chicago, at Gecht's request, to meet with him. By this point she was convinced that Robin was no good Samaritan, that there was something evil in the young man, that he knew exactly where her daughter was, and that he had something to do with hiding her. She hated the smooth-talking little man, but she was terrified about Lisa and willing to talk to anyone who could help find her.

Gecht took Mrs. Miller to another young woman's apartment just down the street from his house. Andy Kokoraleis was there, but he and everybody else denied knowing anything about Lisa's whereabouts.

Back at Gecht's house on McVicker, Mrs. Miller, an intelligent, articulate woman, stood on the front porch and talked with Robin. He continued to tell her he knew nothing about Lisa's disappearance, but would try to help her find her daughter.

"I found myself nodding and agreeing with him and feeling soothed and full of trust," she said. "Then, all of a sudden, I took a step back and shook my head. This guy was hypnotizing me! I hated this man, I knew he had my Lisa, or he knew where she was, and yet I'd been falling under his spell. He had a way of looking deep into your eyes while he talked on and on, and it just—hypnotized you, made you believe anything he said. And me a trained nurse!"

Mrs. Miller left Gecht's house that day and called the Chicago Police Youth Division. They said that while it was strictly a Lombard case, since that's where Lisa had run away from, they would look into it. Mrs. Miller then called the young woman whose apartment she had just visited. The girl was evasive, but she told Mrs. Miller that if Lisa was involved with Robin Gecht, Mrs. Miller should do anything she had to do to get Lisa away from him.

"Why?" she asked.

"He's evil," the girl said. "That's all I can say about it. But please listen to me, and please believe what I'm telling you, that man is evil. You better get your daughter away from him while you still can."

The next day, Robin Gecht called Mrs. Miller and warned her, in a cold, vicious voice: "Get the police off my back."

Mrs. Miller was not daunted. "I want my daughter."

A short time later, Lisa came home.

After the detectives talked with Mrs. Miller, they talked to her daughter. Lisa told them that she had met Robin Gecht and his wife at the Kokoraleis town house during the Christmas holidays in 1981. Late in January, she and Elizabeth decided to run away, and Elizabeth took her to a friend's apartment just down the street from Robin Gecht's house. This friend called Robin and he came and took the girls home with him. Though Elizabeth went home with her father the next day, Lisa stayed at the Gecht house for the next week. When her mother began coming around, Robin took her to stay with one of his girlfriends in Berwyn. She stayed there for three weeks. She saw Andy constantly during this time. Finally, Robin came by and told her the police were closing in on him and she had to go home.

Lisa said that at the Gecht home she'd seen two rifles and a handgun. Robin kept them in his bedroom, which was normally locked. She also said there were dozens of bottles of pills and drugs, also kept in Robin's bedroom. Lisa told the detectives that Robin had two subscription channels on his TV and constantly watched "gore" movies. She said he seemed to "have a fetish about large-breasted women." Robin had tried to hug and kiss her several times while she was at his house, and once he approached her with a pair of handcuffs, but she rebuffed him, frightened. He told her he was "only kidding around," and he didn't bother her again.

Lisa talked about her sexual relationship with Andy Kokoraleis. He was unable to perform normally, she said, and in fact never instigated sex. He would try to go along when she insisted, but the outcome was never satisfactory. Instead, Andy liked being held against her large breasts and cuddled.

"Andy's mother had died when he was eleven years old," Lisa said. "He never got over it. He talked about his mother all the time. He said his father was very old-country, kind of cold and strict. Andy missed his mother. He wanted a mother. I felt sorry for him."

Lisa closed her statement by saying that in her dealings with them, Robin always seemed to be in control and was the obvious leader among the group. She said that Andy always seemed somewhat afraid of Gecht, but that he respected him, too. In fact, Lisa said, Andy would talk to her about Robin as though Robin were some kind of magical, powerful superhuman.

"Actually, I was kind of disappointed the first time I met Robin Gecht," Lisa says. "From Andy's build-up, I was expecting Robin Gecht to be this really awesome dude. Instead, he just seemed like some kind of creepy little weasel."

Next, the detectives interviewed a teenage girl who had baby-sat for the Gecht children. The girl said she was ordered never to go up into the attic, but that as soon as she was alone with the kids, she tried anyway. But, she said, there was always "big slabs of plywood" nailed over the door. She said that Robin seemed captivated with talk about women with big breasts, and that he also had a deep interest in what she called "slasher flicks." He watched them all the time, she said, his favorite being *Texas Chainsaw Massacre.*

As the interviews continued, a picture was emerging of a seriously deranged man who was leading two very different lives.

Following up on leads, the detectives talked to Greg, a twenty-year-old man who had been described by an informant as a friend of Eddie Spreitzer's. Greg said that during the spring and summer of 1981, he and his wife had been out of work and had ended up staying with a friend of Eddie Spreitzer's, who had a one-bedroom apartment at Belmont and LeClaire. Greg and his wife had to sleep on the living room floor, but they paid only $25 a week and didn't complain. Greg said Eddie stayed at the apartment two or three nights a week, and that Eddie and the guy would have sex on the bedroom floor. Greg said Eddie's friend tried to talk him into a sexual relationship, too, but he refused. Shortly after that, he and his wife moved out.

Greg went on to tell the detectives that in the past year he'd seen Eddie only once every couple of months. He said Eddie had pulled up once in the red van and showed him a "big, dark-colored gun." Another time, in the spring of 1982, Eddie stopped by his apartment and pulled a pair of handcuffs out of his jacket pocket. Greg asked where he'd gotten them, and Eddie said: "From Robin, he has lots of them." Eddie told Greg that Robin Gecht kept a large canister on the kitchen counter, filled with handcuffs.

Greg had met Robin only twice, and he deliberately avoided any further contact because he'd been told by his friends that Gecht was "weird."

Greg agreed to take a polygraph, which he passed easily. The detectives thanked him for his cooperation and drove him home.

When Robin's neighbors were interviewed, most of them described Gecht as a friendly and helpful neighbor. One young man was impressed with the care Robin took of his van. He said Robin was always hosing out the back of the van and putting new carpeting down. He would roll up the old carpeting in plastic and put it in the van to be taken to the dump. The neighbor felt that showed that Robin was a clean and conscientious person.

Finally, Area Five detectives interviewed a fourteen-year-old neighborhood girl who said she'd been a girlfriend of Rosemary Gecht's brother. The teenager said she practically had lived at the Gecht house the entire summer of 1982. She said that Robin usually came in very late, most times around four in the morning.

One day, according to the teenager, Rosemary Gecht was very depressed and said that she was going to divorce Robin. She told the girl that Robin had slashed her breast during sex, and she showed the girl the wound, which was about an inch and a half long.

The teenager said that the biggest problem in the Gecht household was that Robin was continually bringing girls home. "That place was like a hotel," she said, "Robin always brung those broads around."

Chapter Twenty-nine

Some moments in a policeman's life are worse than others, thought Warren Wilkosz as he drove along the rain-slicked streets of Villa Park toward the Kokoraleis home. This was one of the bad ones. It was Thursday, November 11. The traffic on North Avenue was particularly slow, but Wilkosz didn't mind. He did not relish this errand he was on, and he was glad to have it delayed.

It had only been two nights since his last visit to the house. He had gone then, along with John Sam, to question Tommy Kokoraleis, Andy's twenty-one-year-old brother.

On that night they had been welcomed into the modest home by Mr. Kokoraleis, an old-country Greek who struck Wilkosz as strong, proud, rigid, and patriarchal. He was a man who, though shaken by the arrest of his son, seemed anxious to help the police. He moved and spoke like a man who had great respect for police officers and the work they did. It was a deference Wilkosz rarely saw in the younger generation, but often observed in older working-class citizens. They made some nervous small talk.

Tommy's mother had died some years back, he explained. He agreed when Wilkosz said that was probably tough on the kids, but overall he seemed to be a man of the old school, somewhat scornful of emotional coddling that seemed to be today's way with kids. Mr. Kokoraleis put on water for tea, while Wilkosz and Sam sat with Tommy in the living room. The detectives were hoping that Tommy could shed more light on Andy's bizarre behavior.

They sat in overstuffed chairs, staring at Tommy, who sat on the couch. A coffee table filled the space between them. They began by patiently putting forth what they thought were routine questions, but as Tommy agonized over the answers, it became more and more clear that something was very wrong.

Tommy was slow. In fact, with an I.Q. of 77 he could have been considered mildly retarded. Certainly, he should have been nervous under the circumstances: his brother accused of hideous murders, detectives sitting in his living room. But it was more than that, Wilkosz knew, and his intuition zeroed in the moment he and Sam began the questioning.

The young man wasn't being accused of anything, but as the two detectives waited for the answers to simple questions, Tommy fidgeted. He glanced around. He scrunched down as though trying to glue himself to the couch, then suddenly sat straight up, then scrunched down again. It was as though he was trying on various postures to see which one might look the most appropriate. When his father came in with the tea, Tommy nearly knocked his cup over. More significant, Tommy began to lie, and he wasn't smart enough to be good at it. He kept changing his mind about the color of a car, the time of day, little things that weren't important enough to risk lying to the police about.

Suddenly, Wilkosz felt very sad for the Kokoraleis family. Because he was sure. Somehow, Tommy was involved.

"It's the duck theory," Wilkosz says. "If you look like a duck, and you act like a duck, and you talk like a duck, chances are good you're a duck. This guy looked, acted, and talked like a guy who had something big to hide."

So Wilkosz and Sam, realizing that there might be bombs waiting to explode, invited Tommy Kokoraleis to come to the office. Whatever ugly details were going to be exposed didn't need to come out in front of the father. Tommy agreed to go with the detectives. Wilkosz and Sam took him to the Elmhurst police station. There they met Detective Commander John Millner, who read Tommy his rights, then gave him a polygraph test.

"The results," Wilkosz says, "were inconclusive."

Wilkosz was called to his office on other aspects of the Ripper case and did not attend all the questioning of Tommy Kokoraleis. But Millner and Sam did. What Tommy Kokoraleis told them that night was recorded and transcribed. By evening's end, Wilkosz knew that they no longer had three murderers in the Gecht crew, they had four. And two of them were brothers. Wilkosz knew it was going to fall to him to tell Mr. Kokoraleis.

The questioning of Tommy Kokoraleis took place in a small, square interrogation room at the back of the police station. Tommy sat in a black swivel chair in front of a square table while Millner and Sam, sometimes pacing, sometimes sitting, questioned him.

Millner, a tall, heavily built man with fair hair and florid complexion, was in his early thirties then. He is a man of blazing energy, both mental and physical. He blinks rapidly, talks machine-gun fast, and reaches conclusions immediately.

One cop who knows him well says, "He has amazing enthusiasm, but he'll drop something without a thought if he loses interest and jump right into something else. I find him interesting, he's a super bright guy, but it can be exhausting just to be around him."

Millner, who teaches interview and interrogation techniques all over the country, watched Tommy carefully as he questioned the young man.

"There's a lot to it," he says. "You use psychology, you study body language, you read eye movements, gestures, posture. You watch for those subtle unconscious shiftings when the person tells a lie, whether it's a blink or a tic or a wide-eyed innocent stare, it'll be something. And then you keep track of those nuances, without, of course, letting your own agenda come across too obviously."

Tommy began by describing one of the murders he had been involved in.

"Me, Robin, and Eddie went out on a Saturday morning," Tommy said. "Robin said to a girl, 'Do you want a ride?' The girl says 'No, I would rather walk.' Robin threw the car in park, got out of the car, Robin put one hand over her mouth, opened the side door and dropped her in, and then Robin got in the car and locked the door from the inside, and Robin took off."

"Where was the girl sitting?" Millner asked.

"In the front seat."

"Could she get out?"

"No," Tommy said, "because Eddie was holding the girl over the front seat, arms around her chest so she can't open the door."

Tommy then described how Robin had driven to a nearby motel and they waited in the car while Robin went in for a room key. They drove around to the side of the motel, and then Robin and Eddie dragged the girl out of the car and into the room. They stuffed a gag into her mouth and beat her until she stopped screaming. Tommy said he stood back by the door and watched as Robin and Eddie had sex with the semiconscious woman. Then Eddie took out a three-foot length of sharp wire and wrapped it around the woman's breast, tightening it until the breast was severed. He said both men had sex with the wound, and then Robin took an ax to her until she died.

"And what were you doing this whole time?" Millner asked.

"I was trying to talk the guys out of doing this stuff," Tommy said, "and I was in the back squinting my eyes and saying I just couldn't look at this, it was getting me sick."

Tommy told the detectives that they

wrapped the woman's clothes around her and took her out to the car, and from there to a cemetery. He said Eddie decided on the cemetery location, but Tommy had no idea why, since he'd never seen the area before. He said there had been quite a few people in the cemetery, it being a Saturday morning, but they continued to drive around until they came to a deserted area.

Sam asked Tommy to describe the area surrounding the cemetery.

"There was quite a bit of tombstones," Tommy said. "And there was a big monument with a cross on it, and then to the other side on the right in front of us was a . . . what do you call things like that? They put coffins inside of there."

It took a few questions, but the detectives figured out that Tommy was talking about a mausoleum.

By this time it was clear to Wilkosz, Millner, and Sam that Tommy was describing the murder of Lorry Ann Borowski.

John Sam set three pictures of girls on the table in front of Tommy. "Tommy," he said, "do you remember that girl that was sitting in front of you?"

"Yes," Tommy said, pointing at the picture of Lorry Ann.

Commander Millner asked, "Tommy, why do you think Robin did these things?"

Tommy just shook his head. "I don't know, it's just like some people, they just want to leave their mark."

"I see. And what is Robin's mark?"

"I don't know, but I know it was a mark."

The detectives looked at one another, realizing that even with Tommy Kokoraleis's limited capacity for introspective reasoning, he had stumbled upon a truth—that Robin Gecht, the catalyst behind the Ripper crew, hadn't ordered and carried out the murder of Lorry Ann Borowski for any reason that had to do with her personally, but simply to leave his "mark" upon the world.

Millner asked Tommy Kokoraleis if he'd seen any news coverage of Lorry Ann Borowski's disappearance on television or read about it in the papers. Tommy said he had, and he said Robin had seen it, too.

"What did he tell you about it?" Millner asked.

"He just told me to keep my mouth shut about it, and I had a guilty conscience about that, so I couldn't sleep at nights."

"Okay," Millner said, "and you have done some others with them, too?"

"I just done two of them," Tommy said. "That's about it."

As the questioning continued, Tommy became more and more agitated. He seemed to get especially edgy when the questions veered into sexual orientation. He had told the police that Robin was bisexual.

John Sam asked him if he was sure he knew what bisexual meant.

Tommy seemed a little insulted at that. "Robin likes to lay guys and he likes to lay girls. So that's bisexual."

"Tell me about Robin's power," Millner said. It was a reference to a comment Tommy had made earlier.

"I met Robin and it was like in a second I was looking in his eyes and I was there in his ball," Tommy said.

Then Tommy began crying and the detectives broke off the questioning for a twenty-minute coffee break. This, apparently, was enough time for Tommy to think long and hard about the powers of Robin Gecht, because when the questioning started again, he pulled an Eddie Spreitzer. Suddenly, he changed his story to say that Robin wasn't there at all, that in fact, it had been his brother Andy.

The detectives took him over the Borowski case again. This time Tommy substituted Andy where he'd had Robin before. He began bouncing around, as Eddie had done, telling his story one way and then another. Before long he was again saying that Robin, Eddie, and Andy had raped and killed women together, usually cutting their breasts off. But, obviously trying somehow to minimize this, he added that the women were "mostly prostitutes."

When John Sam asked Tommy about what they did with the breasts, Tommy turned his head away. He seemed ashamed. He mumbled something about them being in a box up in Robin's attic. That didn't make sense to the detectives, since a boxful of severed body parts wouldn't take long to make itself known in a small house.

"What did you do with them, Tommy?" Sam asked again.

"Ceremonies," Tommy said.

"What kind of ceremonies?"

Tommy said that Robin, Eddie, Andy, and he would kneel around a table that Robin had fixed up as an altar in his attic. Robin lit candles and read from the Bible. Each of the men took turns masturbating into the flesh portion of the breast, first Robin, then Eddie, Andy, and Tommy. After they were finished, Robin would cut the breast into pieces and they ate it. Tommy said that he personally had participated in ten to twelve of these "ceremonies."

"I couldn't believe what I was hearing," John Sam says. "Could this stuff really happen? I just didn't even know what to say to this guy. Finally, I just blurted out, 'Why would you do such a thing?' Tommy said to me: 'You don't understand, Robin just makes you do things.' "

"I just stared at him," Detective Sam says. "I was in shock. 'What do you mean, he *makes* you do things?' I said. 'What does he do—does he threaten to beat you up, kill you, what?' " Sam could not imagine any threat serious enough to make a human being commit such atrocities.

Tommy shook his head and leaned forward, trying to make Detective Sam understand what had happened to him. Sam had been kind to Tommy, and Tommy, it seemed, was trying to be straightforward now.

"He looks into your eyes," Tommy said. "He looks into your eyes and tells you to do something and you just have to do it." Tommy hesitated a moment, then added: "You be real careful when you talk to him, Detective Sam. Don't you look into his eyes, or he'll get you, too."

"I couldn't believe it," John Sam says. "But you know what, there's no doubt in my mind whatsoever that Tommy Kokoraleis really believed it."

After the night's questioning, Sam and Wilkosz took Tommy to a nearby motel. Tommy was so stressed out that they thought it best to hold him in a place where he could calm down.

By the time Sam and Wilkosz got back to

work the next morning, other DuPage detectives had questioned Tommy. They had shown him pictures of other missing women. Tommy thought he recognized one.

Her name was Carole Pappas, and she was the wife of Chicago Cubs pitcher Milt Pappas. She had last been seen on September 11, 1982, when she went shopping at Marshall Field's at the Stratford Square Shopping Center in west suburban Bloomingdale. She never returned home and her disappearance was widely reported in the press. Milt Pappas offered a $10,000 reward for information leading to his wife's return.

When Tommy Kokoraleis described the abduction of the woman who looked like Carole Pappas, he told about being with Andy, Eddie, and Robin when they picked up a woman in a shopping center parking lot and dragged her into Robin's van. He said they took her to a nearby field where Robin, Eddie, and Andy had sex with her. Robin cut off her left breast with piano wire and then strangled her. They left her in the field.

This new story did not sit well with Wilkosz and Sam. Tommy's account of the Pappas abduction sounded exactly like his account of the kidnapping and murder of Lorry Ann Borowski, and the detectives were worried that if the Pappas confession did not prove out, their Sutton and Borowski confessions would be compromised as well. They were right to be worried.

When Tommy was questioned by Assistant State's Attorney Beuke, he again said he'd been present for only two of the murders, but that he was aware of at least nine or ten. Beuke asked how he was aware of them, and Tommy said that his brother Andy had told him about them. He didn't know if there were others Andy hadn't talked about.

Beuke asked about the severed breasts. Tommy again looked away. Whenever the breasts were mentioned, he seemed to be overcome with shame.

"Tommy," Beuke said, "you've already confessed to two murders. You might as well give us the details."

Tommy described the ceremonies in Robin's attic and then said he had participated in nine or ten such ceremonies from May 1981 through May 1982. He described the knife used to cut up the breasts as "a kitchen knife, eight or so inches in length," with a smooth as opposed to a jagged blade.

Tommy Kokoraleis was formally booked and charged with the murders of Linda Sutton and Lorry Ann Borowski. The Pappas matter was still under investigation.

"I called Area Five and told them about Tommy's confessions," Warren Wilkosz recalls. "The Area Five guys were already swamped with this case. They groaned. How many of these lunatics were there? When I described the car Tommy said they'd used, it struck a familiar note with them. Eddie Spreitzer had talked about using his brother's car on several occasions, so Area Five went back and checked. It was a 1974 Chevy two-door, silver, with a black top. They traced the car. It had been abandoned. By the time they tracked it down, it had been crushed into scrap metal."

And so it fell on Wilkosz that rainy night to call on Mr. Kokoraleis and tell him of the new horrors. When he pulled up in front of the Anzak buildings, Wilkosz sat in the car a moment before he walked slowly to the Kokoraleis town house. It would be some small comfort, he thought, if the acts of vicious children could always somehow be traced to abuse or evil in the parents. But that was not the case, he knew. Some of the worst criminals he had seen were the offspring of decent, hardworking people. Such, he was sure, was the case here. He knocked on the door. Mr. Kokoraleis opened it. He stood in the dim light of the living room, forging a weak smile on his face as if he could change the news from bad to good. But as he looked into the detective's face, his smile faded.

"Tommy, too?"

Wilkosz nodded. "Yes," he said. "He's confessed to being there with Andy and the others. We've just charged Tommy with murder."

For a moment Wilkosz thought the father would remain stoic. He stood expressionless. The room was quiet. And then Mr. Kokoraleis fell to his knees, his hands clasped against his chest.

"No," he cried. "No! Not both my sons!"

Chapter Thirty

In the early morning hours of May 6, 1982, Officer *Ron Sobilsky answered a "man with a gun" call at the Grand-Austin Grill, the all-night diner where Tina would later describe Robin Gecht to Detective Pontoraro.

Sobilsky, a big, tall man, pulled his squad up in front of the steamed plate-glass windows of the diner. Other squads, their blue Mars lights visible for blocks, began to converge. A small crowd was gathered outside the grill, and Sobilsky quickly determined that no one was hurt or in danger. He signaled a "slowdown" over his radio, letting other police officers on their way to the call know that the situation seemed to be under control for the present, and that no one should endanger himself needlessly in a rush to get there.

Sobilsky and the other officers at the scene listened for a few minutes to the garbled and confusing accounts of the grill's patrons, some of whom had obviously stopped for breakfast after closing their favorite local bar. Finally, they got the full story: A very drunk man had come into the grill and began abusing a young woman who was sitting quietly by herself. It was obvious she didn't know the man, but he insisted on making foul and obscene suggestions and would not leave her alone, even when other men in the diner strongly suggested that he do so.

At this point, according to the witnesses, another patron stood up from his rear booth and approached the drunk. He was a short, thin young man with a wispy blond mustache and pale blue eyes. But the big black gun in his hand stopped all conversation. He pointed the gun at the drunk. "Leave her alone," he said quietly. Everyone froze. That's when the night manager slipped behind the counter and called 911.

The man with the gun was Robin Gecht.

All parties involved were taken into the nearby 25th Police District, where the long process of determining the proper charges and completing all the necessary paperwork was done. Sobilsky was assigned to write the case report and prepare the gun charges against Gecht, who was the hero in this situation.

"He didn't seem like such a bad guy," Sobilsky says. "Kind of quiet and meek. A lot of guys who like to carry guns come across all macho and in-your-face. He wasn't like that. He was real courteous, not threatening at all. I guess this woman was really taking some abuse and he just tried to help."

Of course, Gecht had no business carrying a loaded weapon, and he was charged accordingly. But during the lengthy booking process, Officer Sobilsky developed a certain rapport with his prisoner, and the two men found they had much to talk about.

Sobilsky had been recently divorced and had purchased a "fixer-upper" home, one that had potential but needed a great deal of work. Learning that Gecht was an electrician and carpenter, Sobilsky asked his advice on a few problems he'd been having involving the rerouting of wiring. Gecht's answers showed him to be knowledgeable, and the two men began to discuss remodeling problems.

Gecht told Sobilsky he was always looking for work, and since the two men lived relatively close, they worked out a schedule for Gecht to come by and look at the work to be done.

A few days later, right on time, Robin Gecht called at Sobilsky's home and the work began. At first Robin came alone in his red van. He surveyed the job and offered suggestions, many of which were huge improvements over what Sobilsky had initially planned. And his work, according to Sobilsky, was "beautiful." He could fashion and shape wood fitting together with the touch of a master, and he "knew everything there is to know" about electricity. Officer Sobilsky was well pleased with the progress of the work, and Robin seemed grateful for the employment.

Some weeks into the job, Robin began bringing along his helper, Eddie Spreitzer. "I didn't like him at all," Sobilsky says. "I never trusted him for a second. There was something wrong with that boy; you couldn't tell if he was slow in the head or just weird, but he was definitely very strange. He talked real mushy and would suddenly switch from one subject to another, or answer something you hadn't even asked. You could ask him what time it was and he'd give you a weather report. Two sandwiches short of a banquet, that boy . . ."

Sobilsky quickly pegged Eddie as Robin's flunky. Robin would order Eddie about, becoming curt and impatient if Eddie hesitated. On Eddie's part, he jumped to obey when Robin spoke, but he resented it, too, glaring at Robin and making faces at him when his back was turned. Eddie liked to brag to Sobilsky, when Robin wasn't around, that he and Gecht were partners, and that he was buying into the business. He laid out grandiose plans that he and Robin were going to accomplish together. They were expanding, they were going to hire work crews, open branch offices in other states. Sobilsky listened to him, saying nothing, but watching as Eddie scuttled to run and fetch at Robin's direction.

As the weeks passed and the remodeling work progressed, Sobilsky became familiar with Robin Gecht's family. Rosemary would stop by, sometimes bringing one or another of the three Gecht children. Sobilsky threw his home open to the Gecht family, but soon began to regret it.

"Pretty soon," he said, "they were there all the time. I'd come home from work and there they'd all be, kids all over the place. They never had any money, and at first I felt sorry for them. I'd order an extra large pizza and Cokes all around, and I let the kids know the refrigerator was always open for them. But how long can you keep that up? They just seemed so grateful for the time and attention, but they never wanted to go home. I began to dread getting off work, knowing they'd all be there."

Then Robin began telling Sobilsky about his marital problems, saying that Rosemary was threatening divorce because of his nu-

merous girlfriends. Robin bragged incessantly about his prowess with women and
his ability to get money from them and make
them do his bidding. He talked about his
longtime girlfriend, Tina, who had just delivered their baby daughter. He talked about
several other young women he was currently
involved with, and he worried that one, or
perhaps two, of them were pregnant.

Gecht bragged about another remodeling
job he was working on, for a Mrs. Bridget
Ross. She was a middle-aged woman, heavy-
set, masculine in appearance and lonely.
Gecht was turning her basement into an
apartment and said that when it was done,
he was going to leave Rosemary and the kids
and move in with Bridget because she was
so smitten with his attentions that she
would support him and give him anything
he wanted just to keep him around.

Sobilsky was becoming extremely uncomfortable with these personal conversations.
He'd hired Gecht to remodel his house, and
he certainly had personal problems of his
own, so he had no desire to listen to Gecht's.
But then things got even worse. Rosemary
began stopping by when Robin wasn't
around. And she, too, wanted to talk about
her problems. Robin was mean, she told
Sobilsky, he hit her, he cheated on her constantly, and she wanted out. It seemed every

week or so, Robin and Rosemary would have a major blow-up. She would have the phone disconnected, and then, after making up with Robin, she'd complain to Sobilsky that they didn't have the money to turn the phone back on, hinting, he thought, for him to advance them the money.

As the summer wore on and the Gechts' relationship seemed to worsen, Sobilsky felt that Rosemary was dropping broad hints that she and her kids would like to come and live with him in his newly remodeled house, a suggestion that made him shudder. By this time all Sobilsky could think about was how to get these people out of his house and out of his life.

Next, Robin began bringing Bridget Ross around. With her short-cropped dark hair, booming voice, and rough mannerisms, Mrs. Ross favored bib overalls, workman's brogans, and a rear-pocket wallet attached to her belt loop with a heavy metal chain. Mrs. Ross introduced a new element into this unwanted array of bizarre relationships at the Sobilsky house. Just as Eddie Spreitzer jumped at Robin's bidding, so did Robin scuttle to please Mrs. Ross. Gecht even turned on Rosemary and sharply reprimanded her on several occasions when Rosemary disagreed with Mrs. Ross on a trivial issue. Then Robin would brag to Sobilsky in private that he was having an affair with Mrs. Ross, for which she paid him whatever he asked.

By late September, although Sobilsky was pleased with the work that had been done on his house, he deeply regretted that he had ever befriended the doe-eyed little electrician, and he wondered how he was going to take back his household, and his privacy. He began using his answering machine to screen calls, and he simply wouldn't answer when Robin or Rosemary were on the line. When they did manage to get a hold of him, he pleaded previous appointments and promised to get back to them later, which he never did.

Finally, the calls and drop-in visits stopped, and Sobilsky felt at ease again in his own home.

Then, on November 6, the phone rang and it was Rosemary. Sobilsky mentally kicked himself for answering the phone, but he hadn't expected to hear from either of them again. He immediately started thinking up excuses to get out of whatever favor she was going to ask of him, but then he stopped and listened.

Rosemary said that Robin had been arrested and was being held at Area Five for murder—a lot of murders.

What! Sobilsky exploded. A terrible mis-

take had been made. Sure, the guy tended
to be a pain in the ass, with all his money
troubles and his endless squabbles between
his wife and his many girlfriends, but—murder? Never! Officer Sobilsky rushed to his
car and drove to Area Five. He used his
badge to get past the police barricade that
Lieutenant Minogue had ordered to keep the
media and other curiosity-seekers out.

"He can't be a murderer, you got the wrong
guy!" Sobilsky shouted at the Area Five detectives. "I *know* this guy, he's practically
lived at my house all summer. How can he
be this madman killer? I'm telling you, you
guys got the wrong man!"

The Area Five detectives tried to talk with
Sobilsky as officer to officer, but he was so
convinced of Gecht's innocence, he didn't
want to listen. Finally, they ordered him out
of the building. Words were exchanged and
it nearly came to a fistfight before everybody
involved realized what they were doing and
calmed down. Sobilsky stormed out of Area
Five, and the detectives went back to their
caseloads.

As details broke over the next few days,
Sobilsky was astonished. And appalled. He'd
left this man alone with his children. And
he, a twenty-year veteran police officer. Good
God, if he couldn't recognize a monster when

he saw one, all those poor young women surely didn't stand a chance.

Ron Sobilsky watched in shock as newspaper and television reports the following weeks brought a flurry of activity in the Ripper case. The Chicago Police Department put out a special bulletin nationwide, looking for information in similar cases. The bulletin included photos of Gecht, Spreitzer, Andy and Tom Kokoraleis. The *Chicago Tribune* headlined: "NATIONAL 'RIPPER' WATCH SET."

Calls came in. Cases were examined. But nothing could truly be linked to the murders in Chicago.

On Tuesday, November 16, the case took a new twist. The body of a young woman was discovered under the Fullerton Avenue Bridge, in exactly the same spot where Sandra Delaware had died. The new murder victim was nude, her bloody clothing heaped beside her. She had been stabbed viciously all over her body. Police found a bond slip in her jacket. Her name was Susan Baker. She lived on North Lincoln Avenue, and she was a convicted prostitute.

In talking to his police friends, Sobilsky had learned that a troubling aspect of the Ripper case was that each murderer had only gradually led to the next. Robin Gecht had never mentioned Eddie Spreitzer in the

Denise Gardner case. Eddie at first had talked only about himself and Robin. Then Andy Kokoraleis had put himself, Robin, and Eddie on the scene of several murders before his brother, Tom, was also implicated. The killers were like beads strung on a lethal necklace, the threads linking them invisible at first. Now, with this latest murder, the possibility had to be considered that there were more members of the Ripper crew still out there.

The Chicago newspapers latched on to the story quickly and ran with it. It got so that Sobilsky couldn't pick up the *Tribune* or turn on the television without hearing speculation that homicidal friends of Robin Gecht still walked among the citizens of the Windy City.

On Friday another prostitute called the police. She said a trucker had picked her up at Melrose and Broadway and taken her to the area under the Fullerton Avenue Bridge, where he pulled a knife on her. She managed to escape, she said, but as she ran she turned and noted the license plate number.

That same day, another young woman was found unconscious along the edge of the Edens Expressway. When she regained consciousness at the hospital, she told police that a man had picked her up at Southport and Irving Park Road, promising her a ride home. Once she got into his station wagon, he pulled a knife on her and warned: "Do anything I say or I'll kill you."

The man drove her to the Fullerton Avenue Bridge, but then he suddenly became nervous and sped north onto the Edens Expressway. She was so terrified she leaped from the car, which was traveling at sixty miles an hour. When police traced the license plate the prostitute had provided, they picked up thirty-three-year-old truck driver Ricky Parker as he was leaving his northwest side home. Both the prostitute and the woman who'd leaped from his car identified him in a lineup. Parker confessed to the murder of Susan Baker and was charged in all three attacks. He was quizzed at length about a possible connection to Robin Gecht, but it soon became evident he had never even heard of the Ripper crew. His choice of the Fullerton Avenue Bridge had been just a bizarre coincidence.

On November 20, Eddie Spreitzer, the kid that Sobilsky had described as "two sandwiches short of a banquet," was indicted, along with Andy Kokoraleis, for the murder of Shui Mak. Eddie was also indicted for murder, attempted murder, aggravated battery, and armed violence for the shooting of Rafael Tirado and Albert Rosario.

During the same week, Warren Wilkosz

and other DuPage sheriff's detectives and a team of search-and-rescue volunteers searched the fields and woods behind the Moonlit Motel, looking for additional victims. They found nothing.

Chicago detectives, too, were still searching. Sergeant Monroe Vollick and Detective Robert Soreghen were sent to People's Gas Company, where they received instruction in the use of methane gas detectors. Methane is a colorless, odorless natural gas formed by the decomposition of plant or animal matter. It can be explosive when combined with air and is the cause of swamp fires, where the water suddenly seems to burst into flame. Because of methane's poisonous and combustible nature, gas company employees test for its presence before opening or working on gas lines.

The detectives did a search of the huge Schiller Woods preserve with the gas detectors. But it was November, and soaked rotting leaves and vegetation lay several feet thick. Traces of methane were everywhere. Then the Department's dogs were brought in and they, too, slogged through the sodden woods. Nothing was found.

Acting on a tip from a man who'd read the news reports and who said he and his wife had been walking in LaBagh Woods several weeks earlier and had smelled a foul odor, the detectives next went to LaBagh Woods. The man had described the area as about a half block west of the railroad tracks and near the Chicago River. Again, traces of methane were everywhere, but nothing was found.

The flow of new cases was over, it seemed. No more witnesses coming forward, no more nervous kids admitting their guilt, no more clues, no more leads. They would have to go to trial with what they had.

Chapter Thirty-one

August 1984

Does it ever end? Warren Wilkosz wondered. It was a late summer day of 1984, and he was making the six-hour drive from DuPage County to the Menard Penitentiary in southern Illinois. Wilkosz listened to his music tapes and stared out at the highway. The sky was a deep watercolor blue, the farms along the way were green and quiet. It felt for a moment as if the world of Robin Gecht and his kind must be an entirely different planet. But even now Wilkosz was on a Gecht-related errand. Gecht, he thought. It never ends.

Wilkosz was driving to Menard because the state prison was there. The DuPage County Sheriff's Office had received a letter from Robin's cell mate, Rocky. Rocky said he had information about Gecht that would prove of interest, so Wilkosz was assigned to interview the prisoner.

It had been a little more than a year since Robin Gecht's trial for the attack on Denise Gardner. Wilkosz had, of course, been there. He thought about Denise Gardner, a kid really, just nineteen years old. He remembered how much courage it had taken for her to get up on the stand and testify against a man whose heart was made of coal, who was capable of the most demonic atrocities, who was widely reported to have mysterious powers.

Denise Gardner had testified in a halting, sometimes very quiet voice. She described how Gecht had pulled his van to the curb and offered her $25, even though she'd only asked for $20. She told how he'd pulled out a knife and then a gun, and how he'd wrapped a yellow cord around her breasts. She talked about the pills he had forced down her throat and how she'd passed out. When she woke up in the hospital, she said, the doctors told her that her left breast had been severed and the right very badly mutilated. She described her two months in the hospital and all the medical procedures that had been done to try to reconstruct her breasts.

And this, thought Wilkosz, was done by a man who was "sane."

Before the trial, Gecht's lawyers had demanded a sanity hearing, and in February

1983 Robin had been examined by Dr. Robert Riefman, director of the Cook County Psychiatric Institute. Dr. Riefman, in a letter to Judge Francis Mahon, wrote, "It is my opinion that the defendant understands the nature of the charges against him . . . and was legally sane at the time of the offense."

Now Wilkosz remembered a frightening moment during the trial. On cross-examination, Gecht's attorney, Thomas Jordan, had argued that in her original description to the police, Denise had said her attacker was six feet tall. At that point Jordan walked over and had Gecht stand up. He brought Gecht up to the witness stand, just five feet from where Denise sat. There was a hush in the courtroom as she shrank visibly in her chair at Gecht's approach. In that moment Wilkosz saw reflected in her eyes the agonizing fear Denise had felt in the van, the fear that all of them must have felt before Robin killed them.

Denise said that she had never seen Gecht standing up in the van, so it was difficult to judge his height, particularly since she'd been on her knees.

Gecht's attorneys insisted that their client, a "frail, little self-employed electrician," was home with his wife and children on the night of the attack. But prosecutors Joseph Locallo and Robert Smierciak argued that

Gecht was guilty of attempted murder, rape, deviate sexual assault, aggravated kidnapping, armed robbery and aggravated battery, for his attack on Denise Gardner.

The trial had not gone smoothly. The day after Denise's testimony one of Robin's lawyers noticed a juror carrying a newspaper with the headline "WOMAN, 19, RELATES 'RIPPER ATTACK.' " Gecht's lawyers demanded a mistrial. Judge Mahon questioned each of the jurors, and two women admitted that they had been following news reports on the case. The woman with the newspaper told the judge she always picked up the *Chicago Tribune* in the morning and had simply forgotten the judge's admonition.

The newspaper she carried had a story in it about Robin Gecht's depressing childhood. The reporter described going to Gecht's parents' home on North Spaulding, with its unkempt lawn and closed-in appearance and its faded red plastic flowers stuck in the ground in front of the house.

The story in itself was not especially damaging, but Judge Mahon declared a mistrial. "Two jurors disobeyed my orders," he said curtly. "Mistrial granted." Clearly angry, he drummed his fingers on the bench. "Maybe the newspapers have learned something," he said. "If they want to be judges, let them be judges. If they want to be newspaper reporters, let them report what they heard in court, not what they heard last month, last week."

It had started all over again, Wilkosz remembered as he drove through the peaceful Illinois countryside. A new jury was empanelcd. Robin Gecht was returned to Cook County Jail. New legal maneuvers were tried. Gecht's attorneys asked for a change of venue, saying that Gecht could not receive a fair trial in Cook County because of the extensive publicity. Judge Mahon denied their request.

On September 20, Gecht's new trial began. The prosecutors opened by saying that they would show evidence of Gecht's modus operandi by introducing evidence of his attack on Angel York, which bore such striking resemblances to his attack on Denise Gardner.

Denise Gardner again recounted her night of terror. Asked to identify her assailant, she pointed at Robin Gecht, who was standing at a table behind his defense lawyers. "That's him, right there," she said.

The trial continued for ten days, with Rosemary Gecht testifying that her husband was home in bed with her at the time of the attack, and Robin's mother testifying that Robin couldn't have done these things, because he was so weak and easily frightened that "his brother had to do his fighting for him."

Gecht's lawyers tried to intimate that it was really Eddie Spreitzer, alone and on his own, who had taken the van and committed the attack. They said that the lack of blood in the van showed that the attack, as Denise Gardner described it, had never happened. But prosecutors argued back that evidence showed Gecht had washed the back floor of the van prior to his arrest, while leaving other areas covered with dust.

On Thursday, September 29, the jury retired to consider their verdict. It took them just over two hours. Robin Gecht was found guilty of attempted murder, rape, deviate sexual assault, aggravated battery, and armed violence.

Judge Mahon sentenced Robin Gecht to sixty years for rape, deviate sexual assault, aggravated battery and armed violence. Then, he added an additional sixty years for attempted murder, for a total of one hundred twenty years.

The Public Defender's Office, in its appeal of the sentence, did not contest the attack or the first sixty-year sentence, but argued only that Gecht's attack on Denise Gardner did not constitute attempted murder. They were trying to have the sixty-year attempted murder sentence overturned. But in an eloquent seventy-two-page rebuttal, the Cook County State's Attorney's Appellate Division argued that Robin Gecht, after inflicting the wounds on Denise Gardner, threw her out of the van in the early hours before dawn, into a deserted, little-used alley behind some factories where she was unlikely to be discovered. She was unconscious, in shock, and draining blood from the huge wound he had inflicted on her chest.

"He left her," the state argued, "in desolation, where death by ex-sanguination vividly threatened." Any reasonable person would infer, the appellate prosecutor's statement said, that the victim was very likely to die under such circumstances. In fact, the prosecution argued, Gecht must have assumed Denise was either already dead or dying, since he had made no attempt to disguise himself or his van, even knowing she could identify him. Later, an appeals court agreed.

Robin Gecht would serve his full one-hundred-twenty-year sentence. Even with time off for good behavior, Robin Gecht will not be eligible for parole until he turns ninety in the year 2043. Because Gecht, a small-bodied white man, was implicated in the mutilation-murders of black women, he was, at his own request, put into protective custody at downstate Menard Penitentiary.

When Wilkosz got there, he was led to a small, square day room, where he was to interview Rocky, the man who said he knew things about Gecht.

Rocky was serving eighteen years for burglary, indecent liberties with a child, and pornography.

"How long have you known Gecht?" Wilkosz asked him.

"Fourteen years, off and on."

"And Spreitzer and Tommy Kokoraleis, you know them, too?" Wilkosz asked.

"I met them in 1981."

"Tell me about Gecht."

"He's been bragging," Rocky said. "For months. He says he done murders all the way from Gary, Indiana, to north Wisconsin. Reads those detective magazines all the time to find out what murders are getting reported from Indiana, Illinois, and Wisconsin."

"Anything specific?" Wilkosz asked.

"He mentioned the huge rock quarry off Route 19 near Elgin. And he talked about trips to cemeteries. He's got this thing about cemeteries."

According to Rocky, Gecht had talked about a girl he'd kidnapped from a 7-Eleven Store, and he also mentioned a girl named Kimberly as being one of his victims. Gecht told Rocky that he was going to kill Tina and Denise Gardner for testifying against him.

"And you'd better be careful, too," Rocky said.

"Why's that?"

"He told me he's ordered a hit on you."

It was late afternoon when Wilkosz emerged from the prison. He didn't know how much of Rocky's tales to believe. Rocky had proven himself in the past to be an unreliable, self-serving liar who had no credibility at all on a witness stand. Besides, Wilkosz thought, there was no way of telling how much of what Robin was telling Rocky was true and how much was just the grandiose visions of a power-hungry little man.

But as he walked back toward his car for the long drive back to DuPage County, Wilkosz was sure of two things. He was sure that the state would not deal with Rocky. Rocky wanted freedom for his testimony, and nobody was going to free a convicted child molester in exchange for information about a man who was already going to spend his natural life in prison.

Still, Wilkosz immediately contacted the Gary, Indiana, Police Department and the Lake County Sheriff's Department and passed on Rocky's tips and clues.

The other thing that Warren Wilkosz was sure of was the same thing that every detective connected to the case was sure of: There were more women's bodies out there. Somewhere.

Chapter Thirty-two

On April 2, 1984, Eddie Spreitzer pled guilty to four murders and one attempted murder. For the rape and murder of Rose Beck Davis, Spreitzer was sentenced to life plus 120 years; for the kidnapping and murder of Shui Mak, life plus thirty years; the rape and murder of Sandra Delaware, life plus 180 years; for the attempted murder of Albert Rosario, thirty years; for the murder of Rafael Tirado, life.

Assistant state's attorneys Smierciak and Goldstein, noting in their closing comments that Spreitzer was a suspect in as many as ten more murders, recommended that he never be considered for release under any circumstances whatsoever.

Though Eddie Spreitzer was condemned by Cook County to spend life in prison, he still had to go to trial in DuPage County for the murder of Linda Sutton.

Throughout that trial, in March 1986, Eddie's lawyer portrayed him as stupid, weak, cowardly, and much too eager to please. Eddie's mother testified that when he was little, his younger sister had to defend him because he was too weak to stand up for himself. Neighbors told the court how Eddie had been a sweet, meek little boy who often ran errands for them.

But when Wilkosz, Flynn, and other Area Five detectives testified, they described the Eddie Spreitzer they knew, the one who had made self-damning statements about the murder of Linda Sutton.

The jury took little time finding Eddie Spreitzer guilty of murder.

Following was the sentencing portion of the trial. Illinois law provides that if there are no mitigating factors, a murder defendant must be sentenced to death. It is at this point that the prosecution and defense teams try to sway the jury, not with fine points of law, but with an appeal to emotions.

Eddie's attorney talked about Eddie's weakness of character.

"These were not Eddie's crimes," she said, "they were Robin's. Robin hired him, Robin was teaching him a trade, Robin directed him, Robin controlled him.

"He followed Robin's initiation," the attorney told the jury. "Edward did not premeditate and initiate these crimes. They were done by Robin. He did not intend for these people to be killed. I asked Edward why he stayed with Robin, and he said he had nowhere else to go."

It was Robin Gecht, the attorney argued, who had dragged Linda Sutton into the field. It was Robin Gecht whose stab wounds had pierced all the way through Linda Sutton's major organs, from front to back. It was Robin Gecht, not Eddie Spreitzer, who had killed Linda Sutton.

Eddie Spreitzer should not be put to death, Eddie's attorney said. He was doing well in prison. She told the jury that Eddie cut the grass, fixed small motors, did kitchen work. He was, she said, a good prisoner.

Prosecutor Brian Telander's rebuttal was explosive.

"Nonsense!" he told the jury. "Eddie Spreitzer isn't a cute little boy who goes over and delivers the sugar to his neighbors. He is a man, a twenty-five-year-old person who rapes and murders citizens of this community! Over and over and over and over and over again. He is a cute little boy who shoves ax handles up women's vaginas while they're still alive, cuts their breasts off, and sticks his penis in those cuts. That's what Eddie Spreitzer is!

"Eddie Spreitzer heard Linda Sutton yelling, 'Help! Oh, my God, what are you doing to me!' And what does the cute little neighbor boy from down the street do? He runs to get a wire and he cuts off her other breast!"

Telander, an attractive, intense figure, paced back and forth in front of the jury.

"I hope you didn't come in here expecting Mr. Spreitzer to be a hundred percent normal," he said. "Normal people don't rape. Normal people don't murder. We don't have to prove he's smart, because if we did, we couldn't do it. He's just like all the other guys in the penitentiary. He's out for Edward Spreitzer. He takes what he wants. He is concerned about his desires, his needs. Just like Gecht, just like Tom Kokoraleis, just like Andy Kokoraleis. None of them are bright, but it doesn't matter. They are vicious. They are vile."

Telander reminded the jury that Eddie had a cell mate to talk to, a TV to watch, magazines to read, nutritious meals, medical care, and access to a telephone so he could call his mother every day. He paused, looked down. Then he looked at the jurors and asked them: "Do you think Lorry Borowski would like to watch TV today? Do you think Shui Mak would like to read a few magazines? Do you think their mothers would like to call them on the phone every day?

"What kind of man," Telander asked quietly, "would hold Mrs. Davis around the neck with a sock while someone was shoving an ax handle up in her?"

The jury was again unanimous. Eddie Spreitzer was sentenced to death.

In Illinois, as in many other states, a death sentence does not mean that the prisoner will be put to death. What it does mean is that taxpayers inherit a staggeringly expensive legal burden that will last for decades. Most capital cases go through fifteen phases, before twenty-one different judges. There are post-trial motions, direct appeals to the Illinois Supreme Court, a petition for writ of certiorari, a return to the trial court for post-conviction petitions, another trip to the state Supreme Court for a full-blown appeal, then the post-conviction appeal, then to a federal district court, then to the federal court of appeals, then to the U.S. Supreme Court, back to the court of appeals, or to the state court on what is known as a 1401 Petition, and then back up the whole ladder again to the U.S. Supreme Court.

On December 2, 1991, the United States Supreme Court rejected Eddie Spreitzer's appeal for the first time. He is entitled to travel the same route to the U.S. Supreme Court twice more. At the time the U.S. Attorney's Office estimated that Eddie would have about four to six years before his appeals process would run out. By that time Linda Sutton will have been dead for sixteen years.

On Monday, February 4, 1985, Andy Kokoraleis went on trial in Cook County for the murder of Rose Beck Davis, a vibrant, attractive married woman whom Assistant State's Attorney Joel Goldstein said, "died without dignity."

Andy's attorney, Pat Driscoll, said that Andy had been beaten by the police, that his confession had been coerced, that Andy, in fact, had played no part in the crime.

Reading from Andy's statement, Assistant State's Attorney Robert Bastone described Rose's death. Gecht, he said, had raped and mutilated the woman and then shoved the handle of his homemade axe up inside her, while Eddie kept the sock tight around her throat. Then Gecht ordered Andy to stab her.

Bastone read Andy's words " 'I was hesitant,' " he said, " 'and I did not want to stab the girl so I poked her, put a couple of puncture wounds in her, so that he could not tell I was just poking her. I started getting nauseated. I had blood on my hands and on the knife and spots on my shirt from the punctures. . . . I dropped the knife and I backed up against the side of the building.' "

Detective John Philbin told the court that

when Andy had been questioned about the murders, Andy said he got them mixed up "because there had been so many of them, seventeen or eighteen or more."

Andy was found guilty of the murder of Rose Beck Davis.

Judge Donald Joyce, in sentencing Andy to life in prison, noted Kokoraleis's "specifically brutal and heinous behavior indicative of wanton cruelty."

Two years later, on March 10, 1987, Andy Kokoraleis went on trial before DuPage County Judge Edward J. Kowal for the murder of Lorry Ann Borowski. Once again Brian Telander, chief of the Criminal Division of the DuPage County State's Attorney's Office, handled the prosecution. Again, Andy was convicted of murder.

At the death-penalty hearing, Telander brought in details about the horrifying deaths of Linda Sutton, Sandy Delaware, Rose Beck Davis, Rafael Tirado, and Shui Mak as evidence of aggravation, as well as going over the details of Lorry Ann Borowski's murder.

"This was not a crime of passion or anger," Telander told the jury. "He made a conscious decision to go out, grab young girls, and kill them, just for the fun of it."

It took the jury just over an hour to sentence Andy Kokoraleis to death.

"Andy was much more vicious than Eddie had been," Telander says now. "He didn't just kind of go along on these crimes because he was too weak to resist. He liked it. Andy was an enjoyer, like Gecht. He enjoyed what he did to those women."

Telander says that throughout the six-day trial, Andy "blazed threat" at him across the courtroom, as though sending the message: You better hope you win this one, sucker, or you're next.

"It says a lot about the character of this guy," Telander says, "when you consider that it took the jury just an hour to decide that nothing in Andy's entire life justified not imposing the death penalty."

Judge Kowal set an execution date of July 10, 1987, but that was a mere formality. The long, tortuous appeals process would now begin for Andy.

On October 26, 1989, the Illinois Supreme Court upheld Andy Kokoraleis's death sentence in the Lorry Ann Borowski case. Just two legal steps behind Eddie in the appeals process, Andy has five more years of legal maneuvering before his appeals run out. Lorry Ann Borowski will have been dead for sixteen years.

Tommy Kokoraleis's pre-trial hearing for the murder of Lorry Ann Borowski began October 4, 1983, in the DuPage County Courthouse in Wheaton. Kokoraleis's defense attorney tried to have Tommy's eight taped statements suppressed before his trial would begin in the spring. Attorney Thomas Swiss argued that the statements had been coerced, that his client hadn't been given adequate food or rest during his interrogation, and that he had been "dragged through fields and cemeteries" during the questioning.

But DuPage Judge William E. Black ruled that Tommy's statements were given "voluntarily and understandably" and that they would be admissible at the trial.

At the trial, defense attorney Swiss argued that Tom Kokoraleis was "a borderline retarded boy who was harassed by police and talked into making a confession with the promise that he'd only be a witness against his brother, Andy."

But DuPage assistant state's attorney Scott Day said: "He's guilty because he was present when the rape and murder occurred." The A.S.A. noted that Tommy Kokoraleis had done nothing to step in and put a halt to the torture and monstrous murder of a harmless and innocent young woman.

The jury agreed, and Tom Kokoraleis was found guilty of the rape and murder of Lorry Ann Borowski. Before Tommy's sentencing a rumor began to circulate through the legal community that the State's Attorney's Office would introduce Tommy Kokoraleis's statement about Carole Pappas at the sentencing hearing. "Hearing may bring Pappas statement," the newspapers reported.

On May 9, Tommy's attorneys asked for a delay in the sentencing, saying they were not ready to proceed. On July 17, sentencing again was delayed, this time at the prosecution's request. Finally, on September 7, 1984, Tommy Kokoraleis appeared before Judge John Nelligan.

Judge Nelligan's sentence was life in prison. "This murder," said the judge, "was subhuman. Gruesome."

Before Tommy was sentenced, he took the stand in his own behalf and insisted he was innocent. "If I did murder, I would say so, but I did not commit the murder."

Tommy's conviction was later overturned by the Illinois Appellate Court, which ruled that the defense had been improperly prevented from introducing statements favorable to the defendant. The statements in question, of course, were the original confessions of Eddie and Andy that had made no mention of Tommy being at any of the crimes.

Until this case Illinois law had been clear that statements by one defendant against another could not be used to convict, since they constituted hearsay. That premise is what prevented prosecutors from using Spreitzer's and Andy Kokoraleis's statements to try Robin Gecht. But no law existed as to whether exculpatory statements could be used in the reverse situation. In other words, the law said that even if A gave a statement incriminating B, that statement could not be used as evidence against B, since it was hearsay. But what if A gave a statement that tended to clear B, could that statement be entered as evidence, or was it also hearsay?

Before Tommy's new trial began, his attorney, Thomas Swiss, on July 16, 1987, entered a negotiated plea of guilty. The plea was accepted and Tommy was sentenced to seventy years for Lorry Ann Borowski's murder, with the stipulated agreement that he would not be tried for the murder of Linda Sutton.

Three weeks after Tommy Kokoraleis's lawyer pled him guilty to the Lorry Ann Borowski murder, and amid much publicity, Carole Pappas's body was found in her submerged car in a suburban drainage pond. The medical examiner ruled that her death had been from natural causes, and all the speculation that the Ripper gang had killed her was over.

Tommy's lawyer, coincidentally on his way to visit his client in prison, heard on his car radio about the discovery of Mrs. Pappas's body. He immediately cancelled the visit and set about his next step on his client's behalf. He immediately filed a petition to withdraw his client's guilty plea in the murder of Lorry Ann Borowski, claiming that if Tommy had confessed to Pappas and didn't actually do it, that should be sufficient to show that perhaps he'd confessed to Borowski but hadn't done that either.

The prosecution argued that the Pappas matter was unrelated to the Borowski and Sutton cases, that the defendant was fully admonished at the plea hearing and that his plea of guilty was completely voluntary.

After hearing arguments from both sides, Judge Nelligan denied the motion to withdraw.

"You can't enter a guilty plea and then just change your mind," Telander says. "It doesn't work that way."

Tommy Kokoraleis will be eligible for parole in the year 2022. He will be sixty-one years old.

Chapter Thirty-three

Perhaps it is true, as the great trial lawyer Clarence Darrow once said, that "there is no such thing as justice—in or out of court." Certainly, if society were to place the outcome for Lorry Ann Borowski, whose motto was "hurt no living thing," and Rose Beck Davis, Sandy Delaware, Shui Mak, Linda Sutton, Rafael Tirado, Denise Gardner, and Angel York on one side of the scale, and then put the outcome for Robin Gecht, Eddie Spreitzer, Andy Kokoraleis, and Tom Kokoraleis on the other, it is difficult to say that justice has been achieved.

None of the Ripper crew has ever been tried for the murder of Shui Mak. Shui's remains, her bones nicked and broken, were held for three years because they were the only physical evidence the state had in the case. It was explained to the Mak family that if Shui's remains were interred, it was likely she would have to be exhumed if the case were to come to trial. Devout Buddhists, the family would not allow Shui's body, once buried, to be disturbed, and it was Shui's grandmother who made the decision to let the girl's remains stay at the medical examiner's office rather than risk burying her, only to have her disinterred.

"There's been a lot of patience here, but a lot of anger, too," said Shui's sister, Ling, after the ordeal had stretched to three years. "My parents, they live in an older culture. I talked to them and finally they accepted it. But they can't understand it, really. I can't either. No one can."

With Eddie and Andy already sentenced to death, the decision was made not to try them for the Shui Mak murder, and the girl's remains were at last laid to rest. Shui's sister was relieved that it was finally over, but she says her parents are angry and dismayed at the American system of justice.

"They can't comprehend why those who murdered their daughter were not executed long ago," she says. "Those boys, they should have been put in the electric chair right away. My parents don't feel this system is fair."

Afterword

"No other case has ever disturbed me like this one did. These guys killed a lot more women than the ones we got them for, I know that. We all know it, we all knew it back then.

"There are bodies out there somewhere, young women who deserve to rest in peace in their own graves, and we should have been able to find them, should have been able to put them to their rest.

"I think about all the parents who can't sleep at night, worrying and staring at the phone and wondering what happened to their daughters. They deserved to know, to put an end to it, and now they never will.

"I quit Homicide because of this case."

—Detective John Philbin
August 10, 1991